Leaves from the Olive Tree

An Anthology of Kingdom Perspectives

Dr. Howard Morgan

To Janet and our Girls,
Brie, Mel and the Tiff
"For all the Love you lavish upon me"

Howard Morgan Ministries
P.O. Box 956486
Duluth, Georgia 30095 USA

Leaves from the Olive Tree
by Dr. Howard Morgan

Printed in Canada.

Library of Congress Catalog Card Number: pending
International Standard Book Number 978-09678279-6-4

Cover design: Ambassador Productions, Gainesville, FL

CONTENTS

FORWARD

One of the great works that the Holy Spirit is accomplishing in the Christian community today is that of restoring Biblical understanding of the dynamics of God's kingdom. Ecclesiastical triumphalism has for far too long narrowed the kingdom focus to the work of the Church. This perspective has resulted in personal and organizational kingdom building while God's kingdom has lacked promotion and advancement.

In *Leaves from the Olive Tree* Dr. Howard Morgan has provided the body of Messiah with a valuable anthology of various seminal essays that have emerged from his deep thought and prayer on important issues restoring kingdom perspectives to Christian thinking and lifestyle. His provocative insights will help you recover the mind of Christ, the service mentality that seeks to facilitate and augment the gifts of God in the lives of your fellow believers.

Dr. Morgan is one of those unique individuals who is able to combine superb scholarship with incisive spiritual insight that produces balanced, theologically sound teaching upon which believers can build solid, mature, Christ-centered lives.

Dr. Morgan gives us some valuable keys for restoring the Jewish roots of Christian faith and recovering a Biblical relationship between the Church and the Jewish people. What has to long been lacking in an over-Hellenized, over-Latinized Church will be brought into focus for you in understanding the Hebraic foundations of the gospel of Christ.

These essays also offer sound suggestions for eradicating the Church's historical anti-Judaism and anti-Semitism. A horrible record of persecution against the Jewish people must be addressed in repentance and renewal of a right spirit in the corporate community of Christian faith.

As you read (and reread) these insights, your spirit will soar into the dimension of the purposes of God. Opportunities for participation in divine imperatives will become apparent. Most of all, you will be challenged to deepen your relationship with the God of Abraham, Isaac, Jacob, Peter, James, and John, the God who still seeks those who will worship him in Spirit and truth.

Let us together seek the walk in Spirit that will bring us into an intimate, personal, face-to-face relationship with the God of the universe through Jesus the Messiah.

John D. Garr, Ph.D., Th.D.

INTRODUCTION

In Romans 11:17-24, the Apostle Paul used an Olive Tree to symbolize God's Kingdom in the Earth. The roots of the Olive Tree represent the "rich" nourishment God's Covenants provide. All who receive Israel's Messiah are "grafted into" this Olive Tree, receive nourishment from those "rich" roots, and become part of the Kingdom of God. This Kingdom, like leaven in a loaf, should permeate every area of our life (Matthew 13:33).

As the Olive Tree represents the Kingdom of God, each one of its "Leaves" speaks from a Kingdom perspective to a particular area of our life. The greater our understanding of how the Kingdom of God works, the more we will grow into spiritual maturity and be changed into the image of the Lord (Romans 8:29).

As an anthology, this book represents works that were previously published in different formats. Some appeared as articles in Restore! Magazine, some as booklets, and some as articles on my web site. Because of this, you will find some themes repeated. They are important and the Church needs to hear them again and again.

I want to express my thanks to the people who helped me edit and produce this book. To Dr. John Garr, my good friend and publisher of *Restore! Magazine*, for his generosity in freely sharing his vast expertise, as a theologian, writer and publisher. You have truly been "iron" for me. To Walter & Sandy Fox, for their generosity and support in printing many of these chapters as booklets, and for their friendship and insight over the years. To Eileen Bowen and Court Newton, both great editors, for their prayerful and careful editing and many excellent suggestions. And of course, very special thanks to my wife, best friend and senior editor, Janet. Her red pencil knows no mercy but her heart is filled with amazing love, enormous support and endless encouragement.

I pray that *Leaves From The Olive Tree* will help to give you a Kingdom perspective and encourage you in your growth in the Kingdom of God.

Dr. Howard Morgan

Passover 2001

Atlanta, GA

KINGDOM PERSPECTIVES
ON THE CHURCH

Chapter 1

A "New" Church
For A New Millennium

As the Church begins the third Christian millennium, I believe that we will see profound and prophetic changes taking place. They are profound because these changes will affect every area of our lives as believers. It will affect how we worship and how we pray. It will affect what we pray for and what we pray about. It will affect the way we conduct our Church services, the structure of Church government, and how we evangelize and raise up disciples.

These changes are prophetic because they reflect the ongoing work of the Holy Spirit to restore "lost" truths to the Body of Christ. They are prophetic because they reflect the move of God to restore the Church to her true Biblical Hebraic roots and to the fruit that those roots are intended to produce. They are prophetic because they express what God is saying and doing in the Church today. And they are prophetic because they will cause the Church to be a prophetic instrument in the hands of God that will affect the world and the Jewish people, and prepare the way for the return of Jesus.

AUTHENTIC APOSTOLIC AND PROPHETIC MINISTRY

Perhaps the most controversial restoration that is taking place, and will continue to take place, is the restoration of authentic apostles and prophets in the everyday life of the Body of Christ. For centuries, these two foundational ministries have been completely rejected, purposefully ignored, or relegated to some past historical era. Those who dared call themselves apostles or prophets were typically persecuted as dangerous heretics, dismissed as those deceived by the devil, or treated as deluded self-seeking egomaniacs. Sadly many were just that. But the counterfeits are very useful for us because they serve as a foil by which the authentic can be more clearly recognized. Others who did not use the sacred titles "apostle" or "prophet," but in fact did function as apostles or prophets in bringing reform to the Church, were usually persecuted and martyred by the very Church they loved and sought to restore to more Biblical faith and practice.

Eph. 2:20 clearly teaches that apostles and prophets are foundational ministries. The Church today simply cannot be, or do, what the Bible describes without these vital ministries. Eph. 4:13 states that God gave five gift ministries to the Church. Apostles and prophets, along with pastors, teachers and evangelists were given to the Church *"UNTIL we all come to the unity of the faith and of the knowledge of the Son of God, to a perfect man, to the measure of the stature of the fullness of Christ."* Has the Body of Christ come to the unity of the faith? Has the Body of Christ become a perfect man? Has the Body of Christ come to the fullness of Christ? The answer is obviously, "No." So, why do we now believe that we need only three of the five ministries? Why do we now accept only three of the five ministries? Can three ministries do the work of five? God said we need all five to bring us to maturity. When did He change His mind?

The ministries of apostles and prophets are mentioned in the same way the other three ministries are, as gifts to the Church. Why would we then have thousands more pastors, evangelists, and teachers, than apostles and prophets? The Bible does not say that there would be that many more of one gift ministry than another. Why would God give so many more of three of the gifts, than the other two, especially when those two are critically important to the foundation of the Body of Christ?

We cannot disobey God's clear direction and reject His provision and expect the Church to function the way it was designed to. God has designed the Church so that it cannot function as the Body of Christ without authentic apostolic and prophetic ministry. He would not design the Body of Christ to function in a specific way and then not provide all that is necessary for healthy functioning, would He? Of course not. So what happened to our apostles and prophets? Could it be that we have been deceived into thinking that the Church today functions the way it is supposed to? Who removed the ministries of apostles and prophets from the Church? Why did they do it? What was their motive?

As the Church departed from her Jewish roots and embraced non-Biblical concepts and theologies, satan was able to infect the Church with numerous "doctrines of demons." He designed clever strategies that effectively removed apostolic and prophetic ministry from the Church. Satan knew that if he could eradicate these powerful foundational ministries from the life of the Church, he could easily manipulate the Church and create a new non-Biblical religion. If the Church could be removed from the influence and authority of authentic apostolic and prophetic anointings, satan could replace those anointings with his own influences. History shows us how satan either murdered the apostles and prophets, or replaced them with those whose qualifications were based not on supernatural anointing and gifting, but on political loyalty to the "Church institution." He also sought to eradicate their ministries with lies like this: "The apostolic era is over, all the apostles and prophets are dead and so are their ministries."

Those with misplaced loyalties easily came under satanic control because their motivations and goals were not Biblical. They sought for institutional position, money and power. To complete the counterfeit, satan craftily arranged for them to adopt the titles "apostles" or "prophets," or another ecclesiastical title that substituted for the position of apostles and prophets. They did not have an authentic apostolic and prophetic anointing, authority, and motivation. They only had the titles. The everyday members of the Church, who were kept ignorant of the Scriptures (by another cleverly designed strategy of the devil), believed that they were authentic because they had official "institutional" designation, approval, and affirmation. But they could not do real apostolic or prophetic work because they did not have the anointing or the Spiritual authority. They were counterfeits.

In order for the Church to actually function as the Body of Christ, and not just merely carry out institutional religious activities, the ministries of the apostles and prophets must likewise function properly. In Eph. 4:11-16, we learn that we need five ministries to be in operation in order for the Body of Christ to come to maturity and function properly as a body. We don't need those ministries just to have Church services. We don't need those ministries just to be Church-goers. We don't need those ministries just to practice the traditional religion known as Christianity, with its rituals and dogmas.

We do need apostles and prophets for the Body of Christ to function the way the Bible describes it. Each of us needs those ministries operating in our lives to help bring us to maturity. We receive from them a specific impartation, a particular nourishing, that only their anointing can give us. That anointing is vital to our becoming a "healthy part, able to nourish the rest of the body" (Eph. 4:16).

RECOGNIZING AUTHENTIC APOSTLES AND PROPHETS

Two of the most frequently asked questions about these ministries are: "How do we recognize them?" and "How do we relate to them?" In a short chapter like this, we cannot go into all aspects of apostolic and prophetic ministry. But it is important to begin the process of de-mystifying these ministries and understand that apostles and prophets do not "glow in the dark!" They are simply men and women who have an apostolic and prophetic anointing given to accomplish specific tasks in the Body of Christ.

Jesus commended the Church of Ephesus in Rev. 2:2 for testing those who said they were apostles and were not. It is our responsibility to examine the motives and the fruit of the ministries. Here are what I consider the most important issues to look for in the lives of men and women who are, and will be, part of the restoration of these ministries. Are they motivated to do things for **your** benefit? Are they seeking to support and nourish the purposes of God in **your** life? Do they come alongside you to help fulfill God's purposes for your life? Are they more interested in building their organization or denomination or network (to use a phrase in vogue today) than building the Kingdom of God? Are they interested in your spiritual development or in your money? What do you have to join and how much does it cost?

Authentic apostolic and prophetic ministers are not interested in your money; they are interested in your spiritual growth and maturity. They are not asking for anything in return and are glad to suffer for your sake. Money, position, power politics, and organizational advancement are not influences in their lives. They could care less about such things. When you find such people, they are worthy of your financial support and spiritual loyalty. They are good ground to sow your seeds into, and quality people you can learn from. Become their disciples!

Authentic apostles and prophets have the same motivation that inspired the apostle Paul, who is our model for apostolic ministry. He shared this motivation in Col. 1:25, 28-29: *"Of this Church I was made a minister according to the stewardship from God bestowed on me* **for your benefit,** *that I might fully carry out the preaching of the word of God... And we proclaim Him, admonishing every person and teaching every person, with all wisdom,* **that we may present every person complete in Christ. And for this purpose also I labor,** *striving according to His power, which mightily works within me."*

Paul understood that his ministry was a stewardship responsibility, **not** for his own benefit, but for the benefit of others. He was motivated by one thing and one thing only, and that was to present every person complete (fully mature) in Christ. He was only concerned with bringing believers to maturity. He understood that this was the plan and purpose of God. He desired nothing else and it was a joy for him to suffer in order to bring this to pass (Col. 1:24). This motivation is something that we can test. The circumstances of life reveal to us the true motivations of the heart. Authentic apostolic and prophetic people are highly motivated for your spiritual growth and maturity. That is what enflames their hearts. When things get difficult, it doesn't change their behavior or their attitude towards you. Authentic apostles and prophets are "glad to suffer" for your sake in order to do whatever is necessary to help you become "complete in Christ."

THE UNITY OF THE CHURCH

Another aspect of this "new" Church that will be built upon the foundations of the restored apostolic and prophetic ministries is that the Church will begin to experience real unity. Jesus' prayer in John 17:21 will be answered. Eph. 4:3-6 will be manifested in a practical way. The restored authentic apostolic and prophetic ministries will bring back to the Body of Christ a passion for God's purposes in the Church. They understand that God's intention for the Church is that every member be equipped and discipled so that he or she comes to maturity. Nothing is more important to them than that. To accomplish this purpose, they will bring a restoration of the Hebraic understanding of unity and how it is practically achieved.

This Hebraic understanding defines unity in Biblical terms. The influences on the Church from the ancient Greco-Roman world will be uncovered and removed. We will come to understand that unity will never be based upon our believing exactly the same things, or interpreting the Scriptures in the same way, or having the same theological understanding of various issues. Unity in the Body of Christ was never designed to reflect conformity to a system of beliefs or understandings. In the Hebraic mind, according to the Biblical model, unity is based upon diversity: diversity of understanding, diversity of interpretations, and diversity of beliefs. When we understand that God is interested in

Christ-likeness and Godly character, then we examine the fruits of our beliefs, the fruits of our interpretations, and the fruits of our theologies. Do they cause us to grow up in all aspects into the image of Christ? If they do not, then they should be rejected. Beliefs, understandings and interpretations which cause us to mature into Christ-likeness should be implemented.

Our diversity is our strength because our differences sharpen us as *"iron sharpens iron"* (Proverbs 27:17). Our differences strengthen us and cause us to grow because they provoke us to prayer and deeper study of the Word. We become like the Berean Jews who, upon hearing the preaching of the resurrection of the Messiah, determined to study the Scriptures to ascertain the truth (Acts 17:11). Just as our human body is made up of many different parts, so is the Body of Christ (1 Cor. 12:12). Just as the parts of our human body differ in structure and function, so do the parts of the Body of Christ.

We cannot say that we do not need the other parts of the Body of Christ that differ from us, anymore than any part of your human body can refuse what the other parts supply. Your index finger cannot say to the pancreas, "Don't send any of that pancreas stuff here, we don't believe in pancreas stuff." If it did refuse "pancreas stuff," the rest of the body would soon start to feel bad, turn funny colors, stop functioning and die.

This is what happens in the Body of Christ when we refuse proper Biblical fellowship with members of the Body who differ in "structure and function" from us. The necessary "nutrition" that they supply is cut off from us and we all suffer spiritual "disease" because of it. If you think through this analogy, you can see just how unhealthy the Body of Christ really is. But God is going to change all of that. The Church will learn the principles of unity and begin to practice them. The Church will come into unity. Those who resist the unifying move of the Holy Spirit will be removed from their positions and be replaced by those who will encourage and sustain it.

Another "disease" crippling the Body of Christ is the insecurity that is endemic in its leadership. Like tares among the harvest of wheat, there are Church leaders who, because of their insecurities, operate their Churches as if they are their own private empires. They do not, or are not willing to, see that their congregations are part of the Kingdom of God and are the personal possessions of the King. After all it is the King who *purchased their salvation with His own blood* (Acts 20:28) and made the leaders merely overseers or stewards of His flock. Because they see their Church as their own personal empire, they suffer from a number of symptoms that prove that they are infected with this "disease." These symptoms include unwillingness to: join with other Churches in city wide events, allow other pastors in the city to minister to their people, support other Churches in their ministry, and join with other pastors to do the work of the Kingdom. As we begin this new millennium, I believe that there will be a move of the spirit spearheaded by authentic apostles and prophets that will bring all local Churches into an understanding that they are building only ONE Kingdom, God's!, because: *There is one body, and one Spirit, even as ye are called in one hope of your calling; One Lord, one faith, one baptism, One God and Father of all, who is above all, and through all, and in you all.* (Eph. 4:4-6)

As the Church's apostolic and prophetic ministries are restored to proper function, and as those ministries bring unity to the Church, so the Church will begin to be reformed. The health that will begin to flow into the Church will cause her to build herself up in love, and grow into maturity. This will be a Church without spot or blemish. This will be a Church worthy of her Lord. This will be a "new" Church for the new millennium.

Chapter 2

Is Your Church Practicing Biblical Religion?

W e live in exciting, significant, and prophetic times. God is restoring the Church. Revival and renewal are breaking out in many places around the globe. All over the world, God is revealing to believers that now is the time to restore the Church to her true foundation, her Hebraic roots, so that she will bear the kind of fruit God originally intended. UnBiblical and cultic doctrines and practices are being exposed and purged. Believers are growing in their hunger for the spiritual nutrition that the Bible promises, passionately pursuing the will of God. Many are extremely dissatisfied with the status quo of traditional Church services. They do not want to be deceived by traditions, doctrines, or practices, no matter how old or how cherished they may be. They are crying out to the Lord for Biblical reality to be manifested in their lives and Churches. And, God is answering!

As He restores the Church to her Hebraic roots, Biblical foundations, and Book of Acts experience with the risen Messiah, the Church is becoming without *"spot or blemish"* (Eph. 5:27). The restored Church will grow because she is being well nourished. She will be busy doing the will of God. She will be prepared and empowered to go forth to accomplish God's purposes. She is being trained to reign and rule with Christ when He returns (2Tim. 2:12; Rev. 5:10, 20:6).

Are you part of this restoration? Are you personally being restored? Is your Church? If not, why not? As the Lord is restoring the Church, these and other searching questions are arising about God's original Biblical design for the Body of Christ. Believers world wide are re-examining their lives, traditions, beliefs, and Churches in the light of what the Bible teaches.

We must be very wise and discerning to be sure that we serve in Biblical Churches that reflect the design and patterns revealed in Scripture so that the will of God is being achieved. Remember, satan disguises himself as an angel of light and so do his ministers (2Cor.11:14-15). Jesus warned us about those who are wolves in sheep's clothing (Mat.7:15), and tares among the wheat (Mat.13:24-30). We must be wise as serpents and gentle as doves (Mat.10:16) as we endeavor to fulfill God's call upon our lives. Satan will stop at nothing in his attempts to prevent us from fulfilling God's will (2Cor. 2:11, 1 Peter 5:8). Recognizing that, we must very boldly take responsibility for our spiritual lives and begin to ask some important and penetrating questions. The first is perhaps the most important one: is my Church fulfilling its part in accomplishing the will of God in my life, or is it accomplishing some other purpose?

A study of the Bible reveals to us that the will of God for His Church is accomplished by fulfilling four basic objectives. A Biblical Church is:

1) **Evangelizing The Lost:** Every Church should be actively engaged in local and global evangelism. Every

believer is to be an active personal witness of the Gospel. New believers should be regularly added to the Church. The fulfillment of the Great Commission is every Christian's responsibility. We are either being sent or we are helping to send others. (Acts 1:8, Mat. 28:19)

2) **Maturing The Saints**: In order for people to grow in spiritual health and maturity they must be in an environment where the Word and Spirit of God impact their whole life. This environment should provide the necessary nutrition for growth and maturity, including all aspects of Biblical ministry such as: worship, prayer, communion, baptism, study, preaching, teaching, healing, spiritual gifts, building quality personal relationships, etc. (Col. 1:28, 2:19; Phil. 3:12; Eph. 4:15,16; 1 Cor. 1:7)

3) **Training The Mature**: As believers reach a certain level of maturity, they are ready for the appropriate kind of discipling, educating, and equipping they need to fulfill their particular ministry. (Eph. 4:11-12, Mat. 28:19)

4) **Sending The Trained:** Every trained member is sent out to fulfill their own call and ministry, whether locally, as part of their own congregation, or to another place in the world. No one should be burying their talents! (Matt. 25:25)

A Biblical Church evangelizes the lost, matures the saved, trains the mature, and sends the trained. This is its Biblical mandate and calling. Every activity and event a Biblical Church sponsors must exist because it is seeking to accomplish these goals. Every individual member of a Biblical Church is, at one time or another, involved in all the above activities depending upon their level of growth and maturity. For instance, you can be maturing in one area of your life while being trained in another. Or you can be sent out to fulfill one aspect of your ministry while you are nurtured in another part of your life. An example might be someone being trained in personal evangelism while already moving in intercessory prayer, or someone might be ministering to the sick in hospitals while being trained in worship.

A Biblical Church's focus is to accomplish the eternal purpose of God. This purpose, as revealed in Scripture, is the maturation of the saints so that they can fulfill the will of God, grow into the image of Jesus, and be worthy of ruling and reigning with Him forever (Mat. 25:21,23; Luke 19:17,19; Col. 1:28; Eph. 4:12; Rom. 8:29; 2Tim. 2:12; Rev. 5:10, 20:6, 22:5).

Our spiritual enemy, satan, and those false ministers under his control are counterfeits and liars (2Cor. 11:15, John 8:44). He will use any means necessary to prevent believers from fulfilling the eternal purposes of God. When satan realized that he could not stop the early Church by persecution, he began his strategy of removing the Church from her Jewish roots, re-planting her into the philosophies and customs of the Greco-Roman world. He realized that he could infiltrate the Church by using these worldly concepts. They formed the basis of ungodly doctrines that brought compromise to believers, influencing and controlling their spiritual life and growth. We must be ever vigilant to discern and expose any point at which satan has infiltrated the Body of Christ (Mat. 13:24-30, Prov. 30:19, 2Cor. 2:11, Eph. 6:11-17), causing non-Biblical doctrines and practices that nullify, negate, distort, or hinder the purposes of God.

These infiltrations have created many Churches that are non-Biblical in doctrine and practice. Not practicing the religion of the Bible, they, in essence, practice other religions. If a Church is not functioning to attain Biblical goals, it is practicing other religious beliefs, and is therefore a cult.

Does the word cult strike you as sharp or harsh? Perhaps it should. I believe it is time to take the veneer of normalcy and respectability off of those "Churches" that are non-Biblical in their doctrines and practices and identify them for what they are: cults. The American Heritage Dictionary defines a cult in a way that most of us are familiar with. It states that a cult is: "A religion or religious sect generally considered to be extremist or false, with its followers often living in an unconventional manner under the guidance of an authoritarian, charismatic leader, also: the followers of such a religion or sect." But the Merriam-Webster's Collegiate Dictionary defines a cult as "a system of religious beliefs and ritual; also: its body of adherents". I would like us to focus our discussion on this definition because it is the one that more directly affects us as believers. Let us remember that both Biblical and non-Biblical Churches meet in the name of Jesus for the professed purpose of doing the will of God. But upon deeper investigation and evaluation, we will discover that purposes other than the will of God are being accomplished in non-Biblical Churches.

How many people who call themselves Christians lack a personal relationship with God, never bear any fruit for the Kingdom or God, and have never grown spiritually, but will adamantly declare that they are Christians because they "go to Church every Sunday"? They have been deceived into thinking that sitting in a pew and observing a Church service is all a Christian does. This mentality is pervasive in our culture. If someone says they are a Christian, the next question asked is: "What Church do you go to?" I think that the question that should be asked is: "What is the Lord saying to you and what are you doing about it?" The difference between those questions reveals an important issue. Are we disciples of the Kingdom of

God or are we practitioners of a non-Biblical religion? Are we part of a cult?

In other words, non-Biblical Churches, Churches with cultic tendencies, and outright cults, can be defined as such by virtue of their doctrines and/or practices which DO NOT create an environment in which every member is spiritually nourished to grow into maturity in Christ, and where every member is NOT being equipped for personal ministry. I believe we should label such Churches as non-Biblical or as cultic, because they substitute other religious things for what God has designed to fulfill His purposes. These other things create a "system of religious beliefs" and practices that are not based on the Bible and do not bear Biblical fruit. It is these substitutes, these other things that we must learn to recognize, and then be bold and courageous enough to identify for what they really are.

This is important for a number of reasons, not the least of which is so that people can see the issues more clearly and make their choices based on what goals they really want to attain: their own, or those that the Bible teaches we should attain. satan has deceived huge percentages of Christendom into thinking that their Church experience is normative and sanctioned by God, meeting His approval. This delusion keeps people in bondage to a demonic system that allows them to believe many things that are not Biblical. It produces lives that bear no fruit for the Kingdom of God. These non-Biblical belief systems and practices prevent them from getting the spiritual nourishment they need to grow to maturity in Christ.

Cults are not only about people who are looking for spaceships in comets' tails, or believe that their leader is an incarnation of God. The substitutes do not have to be so absurdly obvious. In fact, the early signs that other things are being substituted are so subtle that people do not even know that they are being drawn into the false reality that cults create. Let me give you some points to ponder as you think about cultic practices. As we study the Bible and take seriously its admonitions, we see that God has some very specific goals in mind for His children. He desires that we do His will, grow in Christ-likeness in our character, that we mature spiritually, and bear much fruit for His Kingdom, bringing Glory to His name.

The Church as described in the Bible is a living organism. It is the physical Body of Christ in the earth. It exists to facilitate the fulfillment of these goals in the life of each individual believer. Every cell in this body is to receive proper nourishment and support so that it will fulfill its purpose, do its job, and provide what it is supposed to, so that the *whole body can build itself up in love* (Eph. 4:16).

Any congregation that is not working toward the spiritual maturation of each member is, I believe, cultic, because it is working toward the fulfillment of some other goal. It is in actuality practicing a non-Biblical religion. The sad truth is that many Churches are not doing the work of the Kingdom of God. They are not facilitating, fostering, and nurturing the spiritual growth of every member. They are motivated by other things, like prestige in the community, the size of their congregation and building, their annual budget, etc.

The Bible, taken literally and seriously, will challenge our motives and our goals. This is one reason why many Churches reject the veracity of the Scriptures and then easily refuse to allow them to speak authoritatively to our lives. When this happens we have a cult. Members of such congregations, who would rather believe their "ministers" and non-Biblical Church traditions, end up deceived into thinking that they are right with God, simply because they go to Church and put money in the offering plate each Sunday.

People can be deceived on many levels and by various doctrines of demons. But the final result or fruit of the deception is always the same: people are not conformed to the image of Christ; they do not come to spiritual maturity, nor bear fruit for the Kingdom of God. On a very practical level, the Body of Christ is left weakened, divided, and powerless. What we have is a non-Biblical Christianity that amounts to a huge collection of individuals who sit in buildings for an hour or so once or twice a week, observing religious activities, but never growing or bearing any fruit for the Kingdom of God.

Is your Church providing an environment for its members that supports the fulfillment of God's eternal purposes in Christ, or is something else going on? Has satan infiltrated your Church? I cannot describe all the characteristics of satanic infiltration, as they vary according to particular individuals and situations. However, I can tell you some of those that I have identified. As you pray and seek the Lord, He will show you others, particularly as they affect your life. He will also show you how to deal with what you discover.

God is not interested in breaking up Churches or destroying ministries. He is a God of redemptive love and if you are being led by the Holy Spirit, your only motivation will be redemptive love. If you cannot act or speak with that motive, do not act or speak at all. Pray until you get your heart right. Don't let your personal feelings and emotions cloud your judgment. Cast the beam out of your own eye first (Mat. 7:3), then bring your insights and convictions to the leaders of your Church.

Give everyone involved an opportunity to pray and seek the Lord. People who are deceived need a revelation from God to get free. Do not appoint yourself a prophet of judgment or doom. Do not gossip and slander your Church or its leaders. God is a God of Love and always desires to grant repentance and mercy, not judgment and condemnation. Everything He does, He does for the good of everyone involved. He is well able to close and open Churches and ministries. He is well able to grant repentance to anyone. Keep your heart humble and pliable. In that way, you will insure that you are building the Kingdom of God and not being deceived by the devil into working against it.

Characteristics Of Satanic Infiltration, Cultic Activities and Doctrines

TRADITION AND RITUAL VS. PERSONAL RELATIONSHIP

Many Churches teach that your proper place is in a pew, observing and partaking in traditional rituals. You are taught that this minimal participation is supposed to alleviate guilt and justify you before God. What actually happens is that you are forced to be dependent on the "spiritual authorities" for your personal relationship with God. They take the place of Jesus as your mediator. This is the exact opposite of what the Bible promises you. Every believer is to have a strong personal relationship with God and be dependent upon HIM, not on any human organization, even if it claims to have divine origins.

The Biblical Church is people, not a building or an organization, no matter how old it may be. Non-Biblical Churches provide virtually no spiritual nutrition necessary for spiritual growth. This is one reason why reform movements were started throughout history. Tragically, they also failed because they eventually fell victim to the same demonic spirits and strategies that create an "empire of self" instead of the Kingdom of God. This empire seeks maintain its place of power, authority and control, rather than constantly re-adjust itself to keep its vision focused on Christ's goal for the Church.

This constant re-focusing is accomplished through the ministry of the Holy Spirit who uses the Bible and the many-membered Body of Christ overseen by the gift ministries of Eph. 4:12. It is these gift ministries, men and women who function in the anointing of the Holy Spirit, not a professional clergy who function because of office or title that God designed to oversee the Body of Christ. God never intended a clergy-laity distinction. True ministry exists to see every member equipped in their particular ministry. Only when all are functioning in their proper capacity will the entire Body build itself up in love (Eph. 4:16).

Spiritual Slavery vs. Spiritual Freedom

There are many Churches whose proclamation of vision sounds very good. A pastor stands in his pulpit proclaiming his vision to "evangelize the city" and calls for everyone to get involved. This is a Godly Biblical vision. The problem begins when the strategies to implement that vision take on non-Biblical characteristics. People are coerced into doing things that are not part of God's plan for their lives. They do things because they think they have to, in order to support the pastor's vision. This is where the deception enters in. The Biblical mandate of all true pastors is to equip you to fulfill your ministry, teaching you how to do what God has put in your heart (Eph. 4:11-12).

Biblically-based pastoral ministry to the Church focuses, as Paul expressed it, on *"presenting you complete (mature) in Christ"* (Col. 1:28). Part of the responsibility of the leaders of your Church is to help you to find your place in the work of the Kingdom. No one has the right to put you into a place where you do not fit. The Bible teaches that God "crafts" the body together, with each person fitting into the exact place intended (1 Cor. 12:18).

God has not created any demagogues who can arbitrarily assign people to certain jobs so that the work of the Lord can get done. God will lead you and your leaders into finding the place that God wants you to be in. You will have great peace and joy in the place God assigns you, even if it is a difficult one.

If a Church is not concerned with your personal calling and training, but only with how you can make the Church grow, you have a problem. When your calling ceases to be important to your leaders, you have to begin to question motives. Is the Kingdom of God being built or the "empire of self"? The King places great value on the gifts and calling He has assigned to you. The emperor only sees your value as you work to accomplish his goals. What is important to the emperor is how many people he can get into his Church on a Sunday morning so he can feel successful and boast about his numbers. King Jesus does not ask such a person, "How many people were in your Church this Sunday?" but, "How many people were in My Church this Sunday, and are they growing? Should it really matter to you, pastor, which building they are in, as long as they are in My Church?"

Is a person your pastor because he or she preaches to you on a Sunday morning? Or because one holds the title of

"Pastor"? Is this one personally discipling you? When you need to talk to your pastor, can you? If your "pastor" is too busy to even talk to you, he/she is not your pastor, he/she is your preacher. That pastor should be training mature believers to be shepherds who can personally disciple you. If that is not happening, do not despair, there are many men and women in the greater Body of Christ who, though not recognized by title, are true shepherds. If you ask the Lord for such a shepherd, He will lead you to one.

The only vision you have to follow is the one Jesus gives you for your life; the one that fulfills the purposes of God. The only authentic vision for a Church is one that follows the Biblical pattern of evangelizing, maturing, training, and sending for the glory of God. This vision builds the Kingdom of God and not the "empire of self." That is the only vision you should give your life to fulfill. When God places you in a local congregation --and He will as you seek Him—you will know you belong there because there is opportunity for your gifts and ministry to flourish.

GODLY AUTHORITY AND SUBMISSION OR SATANIC MANIPULATION AND CONTROL

Non-Biblical Churches, and Churches with cultic tendencies, will use subtle and not-so-subtle means to manipulate and control you, using Christian buzzwords like "authority" and "submission." You will not be given the freedom to act according to your own conscience and understanding of the leading of the Holy Spirit. If you manifest too much freedom, you become a threat to the "empire of self" that is being built. You might be treated harshly and rejected forcefully in an attempt to intimidate others who might follow in your footsteps. You may be accused of having "demons of rebellion" or an "independent spirit," when you are actually expressing legitimate concerns over doctrine or practice, or following the leading of the Lord.

Such Churches are extremely threatened by individuals who think for themselves, who pray and read the Scriptures for themselves, and hear from God for themselves. Efforts will be made to undermine and eradicate such behavior. They say that you must conform to the group and to the leader if you are going to be "right with God." If such Churches or leaders threaten you with "judgment and damnation" because you dare to disagree with them or attempt to leave them, you know you are involved in a cult.

You must also be aware that there are people who unjustly accuse Godly Biblical Churches of being cults, and their pastors of being "false prophets," precisely because they are rebels who refuse to allow Jesus to be Lord of their lives. Their accusations are merely attempts at justifying their own sin. A rebel will manifest ungodly characteristics such as lack of love, bitterness, gossip, unforgiveness, and an inability to forget the past and move on with God. They will have to give an account for such behavior (Luke 12:47-48).

DIVISION VS. UNITY

Non-Biblical Churches and cults will try to insulate you and separate you from other believers, Churches, and denominations. Jesus is always working towards unity in His Body; satan is always working to divide the Body of Christ. Have you ever heard a leader say something like, "You can only hear the truth from me (or us)," or "You can only hear from God through me (or us)," or "We are the only true Church and I am the only true prophet"? Listen for the word "only." Pay attention to how it is used. It can be a danger sign that a spirit other than the Holy Spirit is at work. Be sensitive to an attitude of separation in whatever form it is presented.

A Biblical Church is in relationship with other parts of the body of Christ and is able to look beyond cultural, traditional and doctrinal differences to see Jesus in people's lives. Your spiritual enemy wants to separate you from other believers by branding or vilifying them and warning you about the danger you are in if you even talk to them. Separation from the rest of the Body of Christ is a satanic strategy intended to keep you under one singular, insulated influence. This is fertile ground for doctrines of demons to manipulate and control you, preventing you from hearing the "whole counsel of God" (Acts 20:27).The Bible clearly teaches that, in order to grow into maturity, we all need what every other "joint" in the Body of Christ supplies (Eph. 4:16, 1 Cor. 12).

We have much to learn from and give to one another. There is great strength in unity, for in the multitude of counselors there is safety (Prov.11:14). Only a unified Church will be able to impact our society for the Gospel (John 13:34,17:21). Satan will try to prevent our attaining the unity of the Body by any means he can. Be aware of that.

LOVE OF MONEY VS. THE LOVE OF GOD

Non-Biblical Churches and cults often revolve around the love of money. Money will be more important than people. Money will be exalted over God and will become a primary focus. God will be presented as your servant, who can be manipulated by giving money to the "ministry." You can get on the $200, $500 or $1,000 prophecy line to induce the prophet to hear a "word" for you. Jesus said, *"Freely you have received, therefore freely give"* (Mat. 10:8). God is not for sale!

Jesus said that money has the ability to compete with God for your spiritual loyalty. You cannot serve two masters (Mat. 6:24, Luke 16:13). Additionally, financial openness and accountability are indicators of the health of a Church. Things done in darkness are usually done so for an evil reason. God's people walk in the light. What excuses for a lack of openness do you hear?

Of course, the Bible also teaches that workmen are worthy of their hire and should receive generous support. If your ministers are supplying you with spiritual sustenance and training, you should be sowing liberally into their lives and ministries so that they are free from financial concerns (1 Cor. 9:7-14). The Bible has much to say about the proper place of money in the life of a believer. I encourage you to do a Bible study on this important theme.

By Whose Authority Do You ...

Self-seeking leaders will tend to diminish the authority of the Bible in order to exalt their own interpretations or their "special revelations and mystical truths." The Bible is only spoken of as an authoritative book when it is used to justify their position and establish their personal authority. When convenient, the Bible is used, but when it contradicts self-serving doctrines and practices, it is dismissed by one means or another. Be very careful when someone or something is exalted over the Scriptures as the final rule for spiritual life. Study the Scriptures. Examine such behavior in the light of the Bible and then pray. If you are convinced that something is wrong, it may be time to discuss these issues with your leaders. Their response to you will be a good indicator of where their hearts are and whose purposes they are really serving.

SEXUAL IMMORALITY

Non-Biblical Churches and cults often have perverted sexual practices, including celibacy in marriage and fornication with the leaders. Paul warns us about those who forbid marriage (1 Tim. 4:3). Sexual immorality in all of its manifestations is often part of the dynamic of Churches when they stray from the Biblical design. When you know that sexual immorality is being condoned or ignored, you should confront it. If nothing changes, you must leave. The Bible only approves of one kind of sexual practice, and that is between husband and wife. God makes no special exceptions. Any statements about such exceptions are intended to manipulate and control you for sinful purposes. God will never put you into a situation that compromises your sexual purity (1 Thes. 4:3-4).

IS MY CHURCH REALLY NOURISHING MY SPIRITUAL LIFE?

Don't ask if your pastor is feeding you. If you are more than one year old in the Lord, you should be able to feed yourself. Your pastor and Church leaders should be teaching, exhorting, challenging, comforting, counseling and training you. In short, your leaders should be your mentors, discipling you into the image of Christ and into the fulfillment of your calling. They should be finding out about your personal vision through prayer and getting to know you so they can nourish its development as you mature. You must ask yourself this question: "Is my Church supplying the spiritual nutrition I need so that I am constantly being conformed, little by little, into the image of Christ?" Your spiritual diet must also include occasional uncomfortable doses of confrontation and correction (2Tim. 4:2).

Are you being equipped to fulfill your ministry, or are you just attending services every week? Is the ministry of your Church providing you with a spiritual environment that is conducive to spiritual maturity? Are you being sent out to fulfill your calling? Are there ministry opportunities available to you in what God has called you to?

Let's be honest though! Are you taking advantage of opportunities when they arrive? Or do you make excuses? Perhaps your spiritual immaturity and lack of equipping is your own fault. Maybe the problem is not your Church; maybe it's you. Could it be that your Church is Biblically based, but that you are not a disciple? Repent! Don't just be a Churchgoer, or a do-nothing believer. Become a disciple, fulfill your calling, bring forth fruit for the Kingdom of God, so that on that day you will hear Jesus say to you, *"Well done, my good and faithful servant"* (Mat. 25:21). Amen! Do you find yourself making excuses for leaders or others who constantly manifest un-Christ-like or un-Biblical doctrines and behaviors?

We are supposed to exercise righteous judgment (John 7:24), and know people by the fruit they bear (Mat. 7:16-20). Do you excuse ongoing un-Christ-like behavior with spiritual or psychological rationalizations? Do you allow yourself or others to be abused by immature, carnal displays? Do you love your pastor or leader more than you love Jesus? That is idolatry. Do you, does your Church, practice the spiritual discipline of *"speaking the truth in love, so that we may grow up into Him in all things, which is the head, even Christ"* (Eph. 4:15)?

Paul understood the potential for rejection inherent in telling people truths they don't want to hear. "Am I therefore become your enemy, because I tell you the truth?" he asked the Galatians (4:16). Confrontation is uncomfortable and can be painful both to do and to receive, but sometimes we need to get out of our comfort zones and be stretched by the Lord through difficult, uncomfortable and even painful situations.

Non-Biblical Churches and cults use the power of position for the imposition of their own will. Jesus said that the greatest person in the Kingdom of God would be the servant of all. God gives individuals spiritual authority for only one purpose: to build up others (2Cor.10:8). The Church of Jesus is built upon loving relationships, not the imposing of positional power. When loving and supportive relationships are built over time, then true loving admonition and instruction (the essence of discipleship) is desired because of the positive fruit it bears. When she was sixteen, my daughter Melanie said to me, "I love the boundaries and correction you give me, it makes me so secure and happy. So many of the kids in school don't know that they are loved because their parents never correct them or set boundaries for them. Your boundaries and corrections show me how much you care about me and my well being."

ARE YOU BEING PACIFIED, ENTERTAINED OR EQUIPPED?

One symptom of satanic infiltration is the attempt to merely pacify or entertain you rather than equip you. But you have the responsibility to choose the kind of Christian life you want. Are you being pacified by the demonic doctrine that Church attendance equals fulfilling the will of God? God is not interested in how faithfully you attend Church services, but rather how faithfully you fulfill His will for your life. There will be no attendance awards in heaven!

Do you go to Church because it makes you "feel good"? What if the pastor's message makes you "feel bad"? Does that mean you leave the Church? Do you go to Church because you "like the building"? What if they met somewhere else? Are you entertained by the song service? Or does the music ministry inspire you to worship with your whole heart? Is the preaching really dynamic and inspiring? Do you forget the message by Tuesday morning (or even Sunday night)? Do you ever take notes (in a real notebook, not on scraps of paper) when the pastor preaches? Maybe, just maybe, God will speak to you through him. What if Jesus gave you a surprise test and asked you to tell him about your pastor's message on the previous Sunday? Do you think you would pass? Could you get an "A"?

Is your Church equipping and empowering you to DO the will of God (James 1:22-25)? Many Christians are spiritually weak because the Churches they attend are not creating an environment that provides the nourishment necessary for spiritual growth. Just attending a Sunday morning worship service will not change anyone. A message may motivate you to change or give you information you need to change, but it will not change you. We are not changed by hearing a message, but only by applying its truths in our everyday experiences. Don't allow yourself to merely be an observer of a theatrical performance type of Church service. Although there is great music and a great speaker and you feel "real good" afterwards, such services produce little fruit in the lives of those being entertained. The "come to a building and be an observer of a service" mentality is a satanic substitute for the life-imparting Biblical gatherings that we all need. We must be involved with others in situations where "every joint can supply" the spiritual nutrition necessary for growth to take place.

One reason that small home groups are so important and valuable is that they can provide a loving, supportive, secure atmosphere that allows relationships to grow. In this way, real changes in people's lives can be fostered, encouraged, and overseen. Loving relationships that express positive input, prayer, and lots of encouragement have tremendous potential for the personal discipleship and spiritual growth of all involved.

The Bible clearly teaches that each member of the Body of Christ has a ministry, and will on the Day of Judgment be called to give an account for it (Rom. 14:12, Mat. 25:14-30). If you have not discovered your ministry, or if you have and are not being trained to fulfill it or are being hindered from fulfilling it by Church practice or teaching, you must take personal charge of your own spiritual life. If your Church is not fulfilling its Biblical role in providing the spiritual nourishment you need, don't wait until you die of spiritual malnutrition.

Like the good stewards of Luke 12 and 16, you are responsible to fulfill your ministry. Find a Church where the sustenance you need is being ministered. Don't be discouraged. God is restoring to many Churches a passion for, and knowledge of, the way to produce environments that provide such sustenance. We encourage you to join with us in prayer and fasting for the restoration process that is taking place around the world.

We only have a finite number of days to prepare for eternity. Let's not waste any of them because of non-Biblical or cultic beliefs and practices. I urge you to begin to seek the answers to the questions raised in this chapter—and any other questions the Lord might pose to you. Your answers have eternal ramifications!

KINGDOM PERSPECTIVES
ON RELATIONSHIPS

Chapter 3

The "Dung" Gate

The Bible gives us the instructions we need for every aspect of our life with God and each other. Teaching us in many ways and on many levels, it gives us straightforward commandments and general principles, using types and shadows, parables and stories. One aspect of the Holy Spirit's ministry is to reveal the truths of God to those who want them (John 16:13). I believe the Holy Spirit has given me a humorous, but extremely important, insight into one aspect of maintaining healthy relationships in the Body of Christ.

It is vital that we understand how the Body of Christ operates if we, as individual members of it, are going to be healthy and functioning properly. Because many people either don't understand—or refuse to practice—these Scriptural directives, they fail to have healthy relationships with other believers, or anyone else for that matter, because these principles apply to all human relationships. This failure is one reason that, for many people, Church is simply a place where religious services are conducted. Instead of functioning as a body, the people are basically reduced to spectators who observe various kinds of rituals.

As we study the Bible, we discover that God has laid out His divine patterns and principles to govern our walk with Him and with each other. If we do not follow these guidelines, we will not have a relationship with the God of Scripture. Our disobedience and rebellion will create our own "religion" with a god of our own imagination. As we learn God's patterns and principles, and obey them step by step, His discipleship process accomplishes its goal of conforming us into the image of His Son (Romans 8:29).

When you are authentically "born again," or more accurately "born from above," a number of profound changes take place in your life. These changes are the proof of your salvation. They show that you have actually repented of your sins and have allowed the Spirit of God to take up residence in your heart and begin His process of conforming you to the image of Jesus. One of the first things the Holy Spirit does is minister to you the love of God, perhaps the most profound experience any human being can have. Without it we cannot really go on as disciples of Jesus.

The Holy Spirit desires to minister the love of God to us and enable us to express this love back to God and to others. Yet many Christians fail to allow this love to deeply penetrate their hearts. Why is expressing love to others so hard? What hinders us?

As I was meditating on these questions, I felt the Holy Spirit begin to illuminate for me a number of related issues. He first began to speak about the nature of the Body of Christ and how, like a human body, it was designed to receive nourishment, to use it for growth and health, and then to cleanse itself from the impurities that were created by the normal healthy process of digestion.

ASSIGNED TO YOUR PLACE IN THE BODY

When you are "born from above" and begin to experience the love of God, some things begin to happen to you. You find your desires and motivations changing. You find your old relationships changing, and you begin to seek out fellowship with other believers. You find yourself in Church with all kinds of people, some of whom you might never have associated with in the past. God has a local Church, or faith community, for every one of His children. He assigns us to these fellowships, be they big or small, for a season, be it long or short. Commitment to a local assembly is very important, because much significant work that the Holy Spirit wants to do in conforming us to the image of Jesus is accomplished in local Church relationships. If God moves you out of one Church, He will eventually move you into another. He will never leave you unaffiliated as a permanent condition.

Anyone who says he is right with God and refuses to be part of a local Church is deceived. Our walk is not a "me and Jesus walk," but a "we and Jesus walk." Studying our Jewish roots reveals to us the spiritual concept of "corporate salvation." Not only does God save us as individuals, but He also relates to us as a "nation" and a "kingdom" (1 Peter 2:9, Revelation 5:10). God interacts with us as part of a whole, and not just as an individual unit (1 Corinthians 12:12-27).

We are assigned to specific congregations because God has specific purposes to accomplish in, with, and through us in these places. People there have, or are, specific sources of nourishment for us. Ephesians 4:16 makes this clear: "We are to grow up in all aspects into Him, who is the head, even

Christ, from whom the whole body, being fitted and held together by that which every joint supplies, according to the proper working of each individual part, causes the growth of the body for the building up of itself in love."

Our spiritual growth and maturity, our spiritual health and usefulness, are directly connected to being in right relationship with other members of the Body of Christ. We supply essential sources of "nourishment" to one another. In order for that nourishment to be provided, each individual part must be healthy and in vital relationship with the Head and with the other parts of the body. Often, we do not know how to maintain healthy working relationships that allow the Head to supply us with the "nutrition" we need for health, growth, and usefulness. We also do not know how - or refuse to learn how - to have successful relationships in the Body of Christ. We don't handle the relational difficulties and problems we encounter with one another in positive and redemptive ways. We allow ourselves to be filled with negative thoughts, feelings and attitudes.

How many people are no longer actively involved in the Body of Christ because of being offended? How many are filled with anger, bitterness and resentment? No one can become a member of the Body of Christ for any length of time and not get hurt. Pain is part of the process of growth. Jesus learned obedience through the things He suffered (Hebrews 5:8), and so do we! What we have to learn is how to deal with our pain, our offenses, and all the other negative things that relationships naturally and normally produce.

God has assigned you to be a part of a particular congregation for a set time to accomplish specific purposes. You cannot leave that congregation before God's purposes have been accomplished and expect to remain in God's will.

You are only frustrating His plans for your life and causing Him to start over again with a new group of people. Did you ever notice how some people always have the same problems? It is not because of what others did, it is because of the issues that God is dealing with in their own hearts. People who are always having the same kinds of problems are people who are not letting God deal with the real issues of their lives. There is no blame shifting in the Kingdom of God. There is only the taking of personal responsibility. This is the key to change, growth, and maturity.

SATANIC STRATEGIES

Satan's strategy is always to divide and conquer. If he can convince you to separate yourself from a local congregation and remain unaffiliated with the Body of Christ, he has won a major victory over you. Like the lion that hunts for prey, satan looks for the straggler separated from the flock. The one that is weak, or alienated for whatever reason, is easy prey. 1 Peter 5:8 warns us about this tactic of the devil: "Be of sober spirit, be on the alert. Your adversary, the devil, prowls about like a roaring lion, seeking someone to devour."

If your enemy can convince you to remain alone, he is able to feed you lies about God, about the Church, about individuals, and about yourself. With no one to talk to about these things, it is extremely difficult to separate the lies from the truth and to understand what to do to remedy any problems. When you remain alone, satan gets the kind of access to your life that makes it easy for him to manipulate your thinking. His thoughts become yours because he lies to you with the voice of your own mind, and so you think they are your own thoughts when they are actually his. You can see how easily confusion can be used by your enemy to manipulate you. Once satan has this advantage over you, it is very hard to get free. You have to pray, humble yourself, repent, get right with God, and forgive those with whom you had problems.

How the Body of Christ Functions

The New Testament teaches us that the Body of Christ functions just like a human body (1Corinthians 12:12-27, Romans 12:5, Ephesians 4:16). All of us are individual members of this body. Our interpersonal relationships are like interactions between the various parts of our body. Each part of our body needs all the other parts to be healthy and function correctly. No part of our body can say to another part that it has no need of it. One part of our body cannot say to another part: "I don't like you. I don't like what you look like, or what you sound like, or what you do. I don't want anything to do with you." It's as if your hand said to your lungs, "Look, I just don't like you, or what you do, so keep your 'lung stuff' away from me. I don't need, like, or want it." In a short time that hand is going to be very sick, and if its relationship with the lung is not restored, it will die. Death is the inevitable result of any part of the body being out of proper, healthy relationship with the rest of the body.

So it is with the Body of Christ. You cannot remain divorced from relationships with the rest of the Body of Christ without suffering serious spiritual malnutrition and ultimately spiritual death. We cannot be spiritually healthy or come to spiritual maturity alone. The deceptive part of this is that your natural life can go on seemingly unaffected. But spiritually, your relationship with God and His Kingdom purposes for your life slowly begin to die. This death process is evidenced by a steady decrease in your love for God and an increased hardening of your heart toward other people and to the will of God. Prayer, worship, fellowship, and Bible study all begin to fade from your life.

We find entire Churches deeply affected by this spiritual death process. Members of such Churches are not in healthy relationships and have effectively isolated and insulated themselves from each other. They simply gather in a building to observe a service or ritual, and then they leave. This even happens in many so-called "Spirit-filled Churches." People have allowed offenses, fears of being offended, previous hurts and rejections, or fears of being hurt or rejected to keep them from entering into authentic Kingdom relationships that define the true Body of Christ. As this kind of sickness is allowed to pervade the Church, we eventually practice a non-Biblical religion that is a counterfeit for the realities of the Kingdom of God.

Just as there is an immune system to fight against sicknesses in the human body, so the Lord has provided an "immune system" to fight against sickness in the Body of Christ. Just as our human body has specialized cells that fight against natural diseases, so the Body of Christ has its specialized weapons that fight against spiritual diseases. The Bible describes spiritual practices like humbling oneself, prayer, fasting, forgiveness, repentance, reconciliation, and obedience as weapons that are effective combatants against spiritual sicknesses. Understanding and experiencing these and other healing virtues available to you as a member of the Body of Christ are absolutely essential for a healthy relationship with the Lord and with the rest of the Church. Without them the Body of Christ would become terminally ill and could actually be in danger of dying.

If you think that this is impossible, look again at many so-called Churches. Have you ever been in a dead Church? Did you see any evidence of the Body of Christ in actual demonstration? What happened to it, where did it go? If the Body of Christ were alive, there would be some evidence of Its life. Study the history of such Churches and see for yourself that the Body of Christ, for all intents and purposes, died. In place of it, a non-Biblical religion was founded; a counterfeit for the Kingdom of God was created, and that is now what is practiced.

STAYING HEALTHY BY USING THE DUNG GATE

As I continued to pray about this, the Lord began to speak to me about the city of Jerusalem. I saw a parallel between Heavenly Jerusalem with its connection to the glorified "bride" of Christ (Rev. 21.2) and earthly Jerusalem being likened to the present day Body of Christ. I understood that the city of Jerusalem is a guide for understanding the Body of Christ. Next my attention was drawn to the gates of Jerusalem. They are places of entrance and exit into and out of the city. These gates are likened unto the ways that truth or error comes into and out of our lives. We have various gates in our individual lives. Among those gates are an ear gate, an eye gate, a mind gate, a feelings gate, a memory gate, a relationship gate, and a spirit gate.

They are the places that we have to guard, lest an enemy penetrate our defenses. They are the places that we have to monitor diligently so that we allow only that which is positive and healthy into our lives. "Gates" in the Bible also refers to places of authority. They were the places the elders made the decisions that affected the city (Prov. 31:23). So we must act as "elders" at our own gates and make wise decisions for our lives.

As I meditated on these gates, the Dung Gate was highlighted as being of particular importance to the healthy functioning of the Body of Christ. I began to understand a spiritual principle. Jerusalem, as a healthy, thriving city was constantly producing dung and, of course, needed to get rid of it. Our physical bodies are also constantly producing waste products. These waste products are the result of a healthy body functioning normally. Every moment we are alive, each of our cells is metabolizing nutrients and excreting poisonous waste products into our bodies. We are in fact constantly poisoning ourselves. If we don't get rid of these poisons, we will die. It is as simple as that. This is why we need organs in our bodies that filter out these wastes and then expel them.

The Body of Christ is the same way. As it functions normally, waste products are produced. Just as our physical bodies, through the process of metabolism, cell renewal and growth, constantly produces poisonous waste products, so does the Body of Christ. As we sit in a Church service we are actually physically poisoning one another. We are breathing in each other's oxygen and breathing out poisonous carbon dioxide. If fresh air were not being replenished, we would kill each other. The same is true in our spiritual relationships. When the Body of Christ is functioning normally, when it is healthy, it will be producing poisonous waste products. When we are in normal, healthy Kingdom relationships with each other, we will constantly be producing poisonous waste products. The question is, how do we deal with this poison that is constantly being produced?

Just as the city of Jerusalem has a Dung Gate, so does the Body of Christ. It is called forgiving and forgetting.

"Lord, how often shall my brother sin against me and I forgive him? Up to seven times?" Jesus said to him, "I do not say to you, up to seven times, but up to seventy times seven." (Matthew 18:21-22)

"I press on in order that I may lay hold of that for which also I was laid hold of by Christ Jesus. Brethren, I do not

regard myself as having laid hold of it yet; but one thing I do: forgetting what lies behind and reaching forward to what lies ahead, I press on toward the goal for the prize of the upward call of God in Christ Jesus" (Philippians 3:12-14).

Just as the inhabitants of the city of Jerusalem knew what to do with their dung, so must the Body of Christ. Far too often the obvious is not done. How many people have been poisoned by refusing to take their "dung" out their "dung gate"? How many Churches have been split, ministries destroyed, and lives ruined, because we did not understand this simple lesson that life so clearly teaches. Everyone in Jerusalem knew where the Dung Gate was and what it was used for. Everyone who used it simply dumped their dung, and returned to the life of the city. No one stayed in the dung pile, or brought dung back into the city, or stockpiled it within the city walls. No one talked about the dung, or kept memories of it. The dung was a natural normal part of a healthy existence, but they knew what to do with it. Why is it so many members of the Body of Christ don't know what to do with their "dung"?

Why do so many believers collect their "dung" instead of carrying it out of the "dung gate"? Why do they insist on keeping their bitterness, resentment, and offences as a part of their lives? Why do they allow life's common disappointments and hurts to infect them with their deadly poison? Why do they spend time talking about their "dung," calling people on the phone to share it with as many as will listen? Why do others sit there and let them throw their "dung" on them? Why do people sit around and talk about all the problems in the Church and how so many people have failed them? Some do it because it provides a convenient excuse for their disobedience to the Word. Rather than getting rid of it, they use it to justify their lifestyle and attitudes. Some people don't want to be healed or healthy; they like being sick or weak. It gives them a ready excuse for their sin.

It amazes me how often believers get together and let everyone dump their "dung" into one big pile so that everyone can stare at the huge mound and exclaim how much "dung" there is and how "nasty it is." They share their "dung" stories, retelling once again how much they have collected over the years, and how really offensive its stench is. More amazing is how many people want to hear about it, asking if there is any more "dung" that they can see, as if what they have is not enough. It is sad how many people only want to hear negative things and are only interested in the sins or failings of others.

Still others want to meditate on their pile of "dung." They spend lots of time thinking about their hurts and the things that others did and said. They should use that time to pray for those who hurt them (Mat. 5:44) and receive from the Lord His grace and love, His healing and mercy. Instead they choose to meditate on the "dung," filling their hearts with bitterness and resentment. We know that they are thinking about the "dung" because that is what they talk about. People who think about the Lord and positive things talk about the Lord and positive things.

There are the people who refuse to let the "dung" go out of the Church. They do not accept others' repentance; they do not forgive or forget. They go out to the "dung pile" and bring it back inside the Church because they do not want anyone to forget about it. They want to memorialize the "dung," and recall it at every opportunity, so everyone will know what happened. Some people have ten, twenty, or thirty year-old "dung" stored up and are quick to give you a sample whenever they get the opportunity. You might meet them for the first time and they will tell you about something that happened to them many years ago. "Look here," they say, "let me show you some thirty year-old 'dung.' What do you think of that; have you ever seen such old 'dung?' Isn't it terrible what happened to me?" Some people have had serious poison in their hearts for a very long time, and their lives show it.

Then there are the people who can't stand it if you are not covered in some "dung." They feel better, or feel justified for their attitudes or behavior, if they throw some on you and get you to agree with them. Did you ever get a phone call that starts, "Have you heard about what happened in such and such Church? Did you hear about so and so?" What they are really saying is "Let me throw some "dung" at you." That's what I call a "dung" call from a "dung" thrower. Some people become so spiritually defiled they think they have a "motorized manure-spreading ministry." They dedicate their lives to infecting as many people as they can. Have you ever been with someone and felt defiled by their conversation, or read a book, or heard a tape and felt similarly defiled? Perhaps now you know why. It is not a very pleasant picture, but it needs to be seen for what it is.

Every day your healthy physical body produces waste products, and if you are healthy, your body will excrete it. If you start having problems getting rid of your own wastes, you feel it. You need to do something to keep yourself free from your own poisons. In the same manner, every day the Body of Christ produces some "dung" that has to be taken out of the "dung gate." Everyday we must repent, we must forgive, and we must determine to forget. Everyday the "dung" has to be taken out of the city and left there. This includes forgiving yourself. There are many people who are being poisoned by their own unforgiveness for themselves. This is a very important and often overlooked point. Some people find it easy to forgive others but hard to forgive themselves for their own failings. We must not fall into this trap. This "dung" will poison you just like any other kind of unforgiveness.

One of the characterizations the Bible uses to describe satan is "Beelzebub" (Luke 11:18). This comes from a Hebrew word that means "lord of the flies." Demons are like flies, and flies love "dung." They feed on it, just as they feed on our negative thoughts, feelings and attitudes. That is why they love to provoke such thoughts and feelings in our lives. It gives them access to our minds and hearts. Once they gain access, they try to exacerbate and exaggerate these thoughts and feelings so as to create greater problems than actually exist. By constantly ridding ourselves of the "dung," we make it that much harder for demons to access our lives. There is much less to attract them to us in the first place and much less for them to attach themselves to. Cleanliness and purity don't smell good to demons!

We must refuse to fellowship with "dung-talkers" or "manure-spreaders." They are the ones always talking about the failings of others. They are always gossiping about someone else's sin or how they got hurt. When they begin to talk about their own sin, and repent of it, they are beginning to get rid of their own "dung," and are on the way to spiritual restoration and health. Remember, it is natural for healthy relationships in the Body of Christ to create "dung" as the normal process of spiritual growth and maturity. Difficulties, problems, disappointments, offenses, and such are normal parts of healthy relationships. They are part of life. How we deal with them, how we deal with the "dung" our relationships create, will determine the health and strength of our spiritual lives.

When we make the mistakenly think that the creation of "dung," the difficulties encountered and produced in all relationships, is somehow wrong, or a problem, or even unhealthy, we can choose to avoid relationships in the Body of Christ altogether. This is a major mistake--and a major victory for your enemy. When we isolate ourselves, we rob ourselves of one of God's primary strategies for working Christ-likeness into our souls. We think that it is okay just to "go to Church." "After all," we tell ourselves, "people will just give me problems, and I don't want any more problems, I don't want to get hurt any more." Such thinking is spiritual poison. It comes from being "constipated." If you are thinking this way, you need a spiritual laxative! Your spiritual constipation is poisoning you. Your soul needs to have the "dung" of negative thoughts, feelings and memories flushed out. The "waste products" of your imperfect relationship with the Lord, and the members of His body, must go out the "dung gate." Then you can return to the "city of Jerusalem," healthy and ready for life. You return to active participation in the Body of Christ, ready for the next level of your calling. You return a stronger disciple: ready, willing, and able to function as God intended. You have learned a valuable lesson that will last a lifetime. You have learned how to deal with the "dung" that is constantly being created. You are able to enter into new and deeper levels of relationship with God and with His Body. You are able to function in a more mature way because you know how to take the "dung" out the gate and leave it there.

When we get rid of our "dung," we are able to return to the "city" and to those healthy relationships in the Body of Christ where we find fresh grace and love from the Head as He ministers to us. We are then in a place where old sick relationships can be dealt with from a positive "dung-free" attitude. Where repentance and forgiveness flow, we can look for ways to bring healing to each relationship. Those who hurt us are not treated with distain but with a necessary caution that tests the fruits of repentance. It is true that some relationships never get restored to former levels of trust, but the hurts from those relationships can be healed, the "dung" removed, and we are able to receive fresh grace for new relationships.

We can find old relationships renewed, or new relationships established, because we are in a place of cleansing that allows the Holy Spirit to change us and enable us to grow and develop new and deeper relationships. This is the result of forgiving and forgetting. We are in a place where we trust the Lord to establish healthy relationships with other members of the Body of Christ. We do not allow old hurts to control us. We get rid of the "dung" that was produced and are ready to move on to new relationships that can prove to be very rich sources of spiritual nourishment for our lives.

This process of healthy relationships creating inevitable "dung"—and then dumping the "dung" and returning for new levels of relationship--is central to our maturing as believers. We grow as disciples because of this process. Like the children of Israel in the wilderness, we have a fresh provision of "manna" available to us every day. This manna represents the fresh grace and every other provision of the Lord that we need to keep our spiritual life flushed clean and able to function in a normal healthy way.

We grow in Christ-likeness as we learn how to forgive and forget and press on in our pursuit of the Lord and His purposes. We meet new people, develop new relationships get new sources of nutrition, and create new "dung." We dispose of the "dung" and return for new encounters. Each time we repeat the process, we grow a little more. Just as our physical body takes in the necessary natural nutrition, so our "spirit man" takes in spiritual sustenance essential for health and growth. Any future "dung" created is dismissed easily, and our relationships in the Body of Christ produce the kind of life God always intended.

The Dung Gate is always open. Are you using it?

Chapter 4

The Incense
of Prayer

When Moses went into the presence of God in the cloud covering Mt. Sinai, he received divine revelation. He was shown instructional patterns that believers were to follow in order to walk with God and have righteous relationships with one another. God told Moses that he was to build a tabernacle according to the pattern shown him on the mountain (Exodus 25:40). This is very important. The Tabernacle in its design and furniture reveals to us God's patterns and principles for our lives. Using symbolic language it teaches us how we are to relate to God and to one another.

It is very easy to adopt patterns for our lives that God has not given. We may even have delusions about God Himself. We can hold ideas about God that are purely the result of our own imaginations and build entire belief systems and lifestyles around them. We then worship a god of our own invention and become disappointed when our prayers to this god are not answered. Then we get frustrated, hardened of heart, and give up our walk of faith. The reality is that we are guilty of idol worship, paying homage to a 'god' of our own creation. This god does not exist and can't answer our prayers. This deception can occur if we are not building our lives according to the patterns and principles set forth in the Word of God.

If our lives are not based on the right patterns and principles, we will wander in a spiritual wilderness just as the children of Israel wandered in a natural one. They refused to follow the instructions given to them. When we refuse to obey God's instructions, we wander also. How many people wander into Church each Sunday morning? Wander through the worship services? Wander into their giving and wander through life? God did not intend this to be our Christian experience. This is certainly not the inheritance the Messiah Yeshua died to secure for us. The present day ministry of the Holy Spirit will fill our lives with purpose and power, not aimless wandering. His ministry in our lives follows the patterns and principles revealed to us in the Tabernacle.

Everything about the Tabernacle relates to our relationship to God and to one another. The Tabernacle pattern is specific with profound spiritual lessons. If we fail to heed these lessons, we become spiritually discouraged and frustrated, because we end up following our own imaginations rather than the living Lord.

One pattern revealed in the Tabernacle can revolutionize how we pray. In the Holy Place, there was a special altar called the Altar of Incense. It was made of wood covered with gold. The wood speaks of our humanity and the gold speaks of Messiah's divinity. Wood overlaid with gold speaks of the fact that we have received divine life. Messiah's life was imparted to us when we received the Lord Jesus and were born again. He is the Righteous One who comes to live inside us so we are made righteous by faith.

Incense was placed on this altar and ignited with coals from the Brazen Alter of Sacrifice at the entrance to the Tabernacle. Incense speaks of prayer (Rev. 8:3-4), and so the pattern of the altar of incense provides tremendous insight into what true prayer is. God told Moses to harvest four kinds of spices for the incense.

"Then the Lord said to Moses, *"Take for yourself spices, stacte and onycha and galbanum, spices with pure frankincense; there shall be an equal part of each. And with it you shall make incense, a perfume, the work of a perfumer, salted, pure, and holy. And you shall beat some of it very fine, and put part of it before the testimony in the tent of meeting, where I shall meet with you; it shall be most holy to you."* (Exodus 30:34-36)

It is significant that the number four in Scripture represents the universality of God's call. Other examples are the four horns on the altar of sacrifice, four winds from Heaven, and the four corners of the earth (Jer. 49:36, Isa. 1:12, Rev. 7:1). These show us the opportunity that God gives for everyone to be saved, no matter what their background or where they come from. The Gospel is to be preached to the ends of the earth and "whosoever will," may come into the family of God. Thus, the number of ingredients in the incense symbolizes the universal invitation to, and inclusion of, people from every nation to pray to the God of Israel.

Understanding the process of preparation of this incense will help us learn God's patterns and principles, so that our prayers can be effective in accomplishing God's purposes. The four plants used for the incense were found by the people in the wilderness and were cut down. This is exactly what God did to us. We were without God and without hope, living like pagans in the wilderness of life. When we responded to the gospel we were harvested out of our old life, cut down, as it were, and brought into purposeful fellowship with God. Just as the spices were brought into the apothecary shop to begin their transformation into holy incense, so we are brought into God's "apothecary shop" to begin our transformation into Christ-likeness.

After being harvested, we are "sanctified," that is set apart for the Lord and His purposes. Having been "harvested" out of our old life and then set apart for the Lord's purposes, we can undergo the process of being made into incense that can be burned upon His altar. We are broken, ground into powder, placed upon a golden altar and ignited with fire from heaven. This is a powerful picture of the process of transformation into the image of Jesus.

Many stop here and allow their flesh and old nature to cry out, "No! I came to Jesus to be healthy and wealthy and to have an easy life!" But it is to a god of their own imagination that they cry. We cannot manipulate the God of Israel to do what we want. He alone is Lord and if we truly want a relationship with Him we must do what He says. We must go through the process whereby He creates "pray-ers." We might try to invent our own ideas of prayer, or meet with others of similar motivation in a vain attempt to produce "agreed prayer."

We can try to "twist God's arm" by quoting Bible verses at Him, but we will simply end up frustrated with no answers to our prayers. It is only as we are formed according to His pattern that we become "incense" and are true "pray-ers." This is the pathway to authentic discipleship, spiritual maturity and real fruitfulness in the Kingdom of God. Of course we can simply become meeting attendees, and givers of time and money, but these activities alone will not create spiritual maturity. Our salvation and the forgiveness of sins is not lost if we resist the call to, and the process of maturity. They are the free gifts of grace. But our maturity, our bearing fruit for the King, and fulfilling our destiny, are the issues at stake here.

The making of incense teaches us God's pattern of discipleship in prayer. First we are cut out of our old life, harvested from the masses of humanity, and thus saved. Then we are set apart for the Lord, we are sanctified. Then, if we are willing, He begins to deal with our lives. We, as it were, go to the "apothecary shop" where incense is prepared. There we are put into a bowl and "ground down into powder." This "grinding" takes place in our daily experiences of life as we walk with the Lord. It takes place everywhere, at home, at work, and in Church. It takes place in fellowship, in times of ministry, in teaching and preaching and worship.

Every experience of our life can be a "pestle" which God uses for "grinding" us into the powder of His incense. The process of grinding is where sin and self is revealed and dealt with. We are put into places of pressure, and preparation. After we are ground into powder we are ready for the next step in the preparation of the incense, that of being mixed together.

Recall that four kinds of plants were harvested for incense. Each goes through the process of grinding so that they can be mixed together. The many, and the different, are put into a unity. Unless this grinding into powder takes place, we are like unground stalks sitting in a bowl. We share the same place but have no authentic unity. We are physically together in the same place, but spiritually we are all still individual "stalks" standing apart and alone. There can be no true unity with those who have not been ground into fine powder.

This is readily discovered when we meet with other believers. It is clear when there is unity and mixing, or when there is standoffishness, religious formality, or any other dynamic that causes separation. We know when we meet someone who is "powdery." If you are "powdery" and meet someone who has also been ground into powder, it takes no time at all to have your hearts joined together and to be able to pray and hear the Lord together.

If we ourselves are rigid, like a dry unground stalk, we must not blame others for our condition. No matter what others have done or said to us, each of us has a choice in how we will respond. If we choose to allow Jesus to work in us and transform us, we will become "powder" in His hands. If we have refused to let Jesus grind us into His likeness, we must resolve that with the Lord alone. Each of us must take personal responsibility for our relationship to the King. Excuses or blame shifting are lies. We might like to take the easy way out, but that is not His way. The Scriptures guarantee, however, that the Lord is ready to respond to each of us individually any time we are willing (Ps. 34:18,145:18, James 4:8, Heb. 4:16). His "apothecary shop" is always open, and the invitation to become His incense is always extended.

Jesus did not take the easy way out. He went right to the cross, inviting us to "Come follow me." He was made perfect through His suffering (Hebrews 2:10), and we can be perfected through ours. Enduring difficulties is part of the process of sanctification, but we never endure them alone. He promises to be with us, and indeed the testimony of the saints through the ages is how present He makes Himself when situations are the darkest. We must not run from the difficulties of life. They are the "mortar and pestle" He uses to transform us into His image (Rom. 8:29, 2Cor. 3:18).

There are people who say they have known the Lord for many years, but there is no evident change in them. Why? They never went to the "apothecary shop" so that the Lord could deal with them and prepare them as incense. They said "No! I don't want to change. It's too difficult, too painful. I'll just go to Church." They may go through the motions of praying and praising and giving, but their lives and their relationship with God lacks deeper meaning and purpose. Their Christian life is only superficial at best. While the trials and tribulations of the breaking process may be painful for a season, the fruit that is always born is eternal and deeply pleasing to the Lord (Hebrews 12:11).

Returning to the analogy of the unground stalks, we must understand that they can be bent, even bent around into a circle. But this leaves them under an extreme pressure until they are either broken or return to their original shape. When the stalk finally breaks, there is a distinct "snap." This is the same "snap" Christians hear within themselves when they finally break and yield to the Lord. After the "snap," your testimony will be like that of the Apostle Paul who said of himself, *"It is no longer I who live, but Christ who lives in me"* (Gal. 2:20). No one can truly mature in his or her walk with God until they have heard the inner "snap." As we go on to greater levels of consecration and holiness, we will hear that "snap" again and again. Only after the "snap" can we be ground into really fine powder and become the kind of incense that offers God the *"sweet smelling aroma of Christ"* (2Cor. 2:14-16). Our old life no longer dominates us or even influences us. Bad attitudes, judgementalism, criticism, fear, lust, greed and all the sins of the flesh will be ground out of our lives. As the powdery incense, we can be mixed with the other kinds of "stalks" which have gone through the same process.

The picture of prayer rising like burning incense can be developed further. There is a difference between praying with people who are like stalks standing together, and praying with people who are like powder mixed together. A quality that powder has, as compared with a bunch of stalks, is that it can be ignited almost immediately. We individually must be prepared to become part of the incense. Our personal wills must be submitted to the Lord's will and we must want nothing more than for the King to be glorified, as our destiny in Him is fulfilled. We will see a new Kingdom dynamic released when we are like powder mixed together.

Being in agreement comes from a particular mixing of lives and listening to the same voice, which like the fire on the altar ignites our hearts. We listen to God to learn what we should do, rather than telling God what He should do. Unground "stalks," simply being physically together in one place, will have too many agendas going on in their hearts to be able to hear one voice and be ignited together. The various motivations will contend with one another and effectively put the fire out.

This particular aspect of prayer is like the High Priest taking the mixture from the apothecary shop to the Holy Place where it is put on the altar. He will only carry the powder that has been prepared and mixed properly, which is symbolic of a special group of people for a special ministry. A people no longer living for themselves, but harvested for the Kingdom, sanctified, ground into powdery incense, offering the Lord's prayers ignited by the fire of the Holy Spirit.

It is a fact that those who are "powdery" can easily recognize each other and quickly enter into fellowship and authentic "incense" prayer, even if they are from the opposite ends of the earth. This kind of "incense" prayer is an automatic consequence of the mixing of such people. The grinding that they have experienced has set them into their place in the Body of Christ. They have a burning passion for their calling and they are committed to it. Come what may, nothing can dissuade, deter, obstruct or thwart them. It is an unquenchable and unstoppable passion. In fact, it is the passion of Jesus is within them.

When we truly give our lives to Christ, He puts the passion there, even though it may, at first, be a passion for something that is impossible to do. This is because He does not intend that you fulfill your destiny alone. Rather, He must do it in you, with you, and through you. His call, by its very nature, is impossible for you to answer alone and so requires that you join your life to His so that, together, you *can do all things*" (Phil. 4:13). This joining of your life to His is what breaks you and grinds you to powder, so that His passion can ignite your life to fulfill His purposes. When you meet like minded people who have had the same encounter with the living Christ, you are easily able to pray prayers that are like incense burning on the Golden Altar.

The fire on the Altar of Incense is taken from the Bronze Altar of sacrifice. The priest took coals from the altar of sacrifice and put them into a golden censer. He carried that censer into the Holy Place and used those coals to light the holy oil in the seven branched candelabra and to ignite the incense which sat upon its golden altar. No other fire was allowed. False fire led to men being struck dead, as in the Biblical account of Aaron's sons, Nadab and Abihu, who did not obey the Lord, and offered false fire (Leviticus 10:1). Only that which comes from God is allowed. Fire fell from heaven on the day when Moses dedicated the Tabernacle. This same fire was used to ignite the incense and light the candelabra. From that first day onward, the same fire was used every day to re-ignite the fires on the Altar of Sacrifice and to re-ignite the oil in the candelabra and the incense. Only that which comes from God can ignite the incense that God creates when he makes us into His powder.

Many people wonder why we do not get excited about so many things that are done in the "name of the Lord." Having paid the price to be broken and ground into powder, our spirits are very sensitive to the authentic fire from heaven. We will not respond to the "false fire" of religious coercion, fleshly agendas, or emotional appeals, because we will see them for what they are: the manipulation of men seeking to fulfill an agenda other than that of the Kingdom of God. When the KING speaks, fire falls from heaven and ignites the powder of prepared hearts!

As the incense is lit, the Holy Place is filled with smoke and sweet smelling aroma. God looks for this—the incense of our lives to be ignited by the Holy Spirit. Our merely human desires and plans, good intentions, intellectual concepts, and ideas are false fires that result in unanswered prayers. Only the Holy Spirit, revealing God's will and purposes, will be able to ignite this incense! Then the Lord will answer prayers in astounding and miraculous ways.

In fulfillment of Old Testament type, the Bronze Altar had been set up on Calvary's hill. Jesus the Messiah had died for our sins, His blood was shed, He had risen from the dead, and had ascended into Heaven. The Holy Spirit was ready to fall. On the day of Pentecost, in the upper room in Jerusalem, there was a pile of incense gathered together in one place, harvested, sanctified, ground into powder and in one accord. The disciples had been prepared and were waiting in obedience. The fire from Heaven fell, and the original fire that ignited that first incense is still burning today. It has been kept burning since the Day of Pentecost and will ignite us. God will not accept any other fire, any other religion, any other services or ministries—only that which comes from Heaven.

There are many in ministry, and others who go to Church, who are not following God's pattern. They are building according to ideas that have been sanctified by their traditional acceptance and passed on through many generations, but have changed from the true pattern. If they are creating their own religions in their own sanctuaries with their own programs, they will not be pleasing to God, and will not bring His Glory.

We must go back to God's original pattern revealed in the Tabernacle. We must allow ourselves to be harvested, sanctified, ground into powder and wait for the fire of the Holy Spirit to ignite us. Then we will see the difference between simply praying because we see a need, and praying because we are on fire and burning with the Spirit.

God is looking for people who are willing to be "incense on the altar." Are you such a person?

Chapter 5

The "Beit Midrash": Learning How to Learn Together

Attached to every synagogue is a place devoted to the study of sacred writings and Holy Scripture. This area is called the Beit Midrash, the house of learning or study. Midrash literally means "investigation." Here the Jewish people of would gather to investigate, study, learn, and argue the meanings and proper applications of their revered texts. In this environment, rich spiritual opportunities for learning are given to the participants that can never be obtained alone, or by simply listening to a lecturer give his or her own opinions.

The opportunity to express one's own thoughts and feelings, and engage in what is often very passionate and heated debate is a very stimulating intellectual and spiritual experience. It is also an extremely necessary and vital part of studying the Word of God, and growing in your personal relationship with the Lord. Without it the opportunities for *"iron to sharpen iron"* (Prov.27:17) will be limited and spiritual growth stunted. Being part of a Beit Midrash can literally transform not only the way you learn the Scriptures but your personal relationship with the Lord.

The dynamic that learning together brings is one of the missing vital ingredients in most Churches that follow a Greco-Roman rather than the scriptural Hebraic model. If these expressions are foreign to you, let me try to define them. When the Church rejected her Jewish roots (and then the Jewish people) and opted instead for a root system in Greek philosophical thought, she lost all the sources of spiritual nourishment that those roots were intended by God to provide. One of the sources of nourishment is this Hebraic model of learning together, which we will call the Beit Midrash style of Bible study.

The Greco-Roman model, which most Churches basically follow, tends to foster a clergy-laity division that, directly or indirectly, advertently or inadvertently, suppresses or minimizes individual spiritual growth and maturity. People tend to observe the "theater" of religious services, rather than be trained to actually partake in ministry. "Anointed" leaders perform their sacred duties, while "lay" people merely sit and observe the proceedings, or, at best, are given very subordinate roles. Those who sense a call to ministry typically are sent off to study in the relative sterility of academically, rather than ministerially, focused Bible schools and seminaries instead of being mentored, discipled, and trained by spiritual fathers and mothers as they deal with the realities of everyday life in the local setting.

This model also tends to minimize the place of learning, because learning is the key to knowledge, growth and power. The learning that is allowed to take place is that which is limited to local Church and/or denominational doctrine. The "we believe this and they don't" mentality is accentuated and fostered. How many people have been told "we don't believe that in this Church, and if you believe that you should leave or keep it to yourself." In other words, there are subjects whose study is forbidden. This sounds to me like the dictates of a Caesar, not the commands of Christ to study the Word of God (Deut. 11:19, 1 Tim 2:15).

This clergy-laity division is not always intentional or even done consciously. Many pastors are frustrated that their people are not growing and doing more. By far the great majority of pastors are sincere men and women of God earnestly seeking the Lord for ways and means to effectively minister to their people so they will grow in their faith. The fault lies in the model in which we have been trained and involves the cultural dynamics that influence everyone. The people in the congregation have a mentality that fosters their own spiritual immaturity by insisting that the Church be run in a certain way. Many people just don't want to grow spiritually; they are happy to be spectators.

I believe that God is looking for people who want to break out of old stereotypical ways of doing things, explore what their Jewish roots offer them, and pray and see if the Lord will lead them to try new things. The Beit Midrash is part of the Hebraic model for the Church that has been lost to us through the centuries. Will you be part of its restoration?

The Beit Midrash is not your typical Bible discussion group that has a group leader, a workbook, fixed agenda, and doctrinal correctness. It is a very free-flowing, open, and often passionate environment geared to giving people maximum freedom to think, feel, and express their views. Yes, it is true that some will advocate heretical and strange doctrines. First Corinthians 11:19 says that it is important that they do – so that those who are approved can be clearly seen. Others will proclaim bizarre revelations, obscure interpretations and weird applications of the Bible. Doctrines of demons will try to make inroads (so what else is new?), and lots more "stuff" will surface at your Beit Midrash.

But, the Holy Spirit will also minister His authentic revelations and impart life-changing truths. Rich spiritual nourishment will be supplied by the Head of the Body. People will have opportunities to be challenged to earnestly study the Word for themselves, and thereby truly grow and change. All the negative "stuff" will be exposed to the light of serious study, examined thoroughly, and disposed of forever. 1 Thess. 5:21 and 1 John 4:1 will be key verses for everyone who studies this way: "Test all things, hold fast to that which is good" and "Believe not every spirit but test them …"

In order to have an effective Beit Midrash, everyone who attends must have the same basic motivation. It is not, as some think, the attainment of knowledge for knowledge's sake or the seeking of an opportunity to show how much they know, but a sincerely heartfelt desire to deepen their personal relationship with the Lord and be changed into His image (Rom. 8:29, 2Cor. 3:18). Developing keener interpersonal relationships with other members of the study group can happen as a result of studying together but is not a primary motivation. Every member of the study group must come with the same motivation for times of study to prove fruitful instead of mere intellectual ramblings or the strutting of egos.

Other motivations will be clearly revealed in due time. One of the marvelous benefits of this kind of study is that Hebrews 4:12 is seen in operation: "The thoughts and intents of the heart are revealed." Self revelation, which is the beginning of true repentance by which we receive grace to change, is one of the fruits of this kind of study. What a wonderful thought for those who truly are His disciples and want to change into His image!

The Beit Midrash model is designed to enhance the spiritual life of sincere disciples of the Kingdom of God. A disciple, simply defined, is someone who honestly wants to learn, grow, and change into the image of the Lord. They are not focused on themselves, or on their reputations, or on how others perceive them; they truly want to deepen their relationship with the Lord and change into His likeness. The Beit Midrash is not about convincing others of the rightness of your interpretations or the erroneousness of theirs. It is about opening your heart to the work of the Holy Spirit so that you can learn, grow, and change.

The dynamic of sharing the insights and truths you have learned, and receiving the same from others, will be a rich source for spiritual growth. These study times will test the sincerity of our motivation, our patience and tolerance for others who hold different views, and our desire to see everyone grow in the truth that God gives them. The Beit Midrash presents to us those wonderfully difficult moments where we have a divinely given choice to act in our old nature or quietly open our spirit to the loving ministry of the Holy Spirit and allow Him to change us, or at least show us places where we need to change. From there we can get alone with the Lord and let him do His work of transformation in us. That is, if we want to!

Let's look at some practical ways we can get started in forming our own Beit Midrash. The first thing you need to understand is that the leader of this kind of study does not need to have all the answers, or any of the answers, for that matter. This is one reason why some pastors are hesitant to get involved with this kind of study. They are in the old Greco-Roman model that dictates to them that they have to have all the answers to everyone's questions, an absurd position for anyone to think they have to be in.

A pastor who leads a Beit Midrash simply comes as a student with other students. He does not come to necessarily give answers, but to ask questions, to learn, to grow, to change. He, as well as the more mature members of the study group, will naturally have more to share from the depths of their experience and years of study. The attitude that you are merely a student in the "School of the Spirit" (whether at a beginner or advanced level) is wonderfully freeing. There is so much liberty in being able to say "I don't know; let's study that some more." We come to the Beit Midrash to learn from whosoever the Lord chooses to use. I have personally learned much from the insights of children and new believers. The freshness they bring to their understanding of the Word and to their relationship with the Lord is always very stimulating.

If you want to start this kind of a study, see yourself simply as a facilitator (to use a modern term) of the discussion, someone who can keep some semblance of order and who is given authority by the group to end arguments when it becomes profitable to do so. Some disagreements are good because they stimulate more study. Others are counterproductive: for example, those immature emotional outbursts that lead to personal criticism, or manifesting such emotional manipulation such as ignoring someone or sulking. The levels of spiritual and emotional maturity of those in the study group will determine how much disagreement they can handle. As people learn how to participate in this kind of study, they will be able to handle more and more "Godly friction." You will also learn more about facilitating as you lead more meetings. This is also part of the joy of learning. It happens on every level.

Remember, learning is what this Beit Midrash experience is all about. You can't fail at this because it is all about learning, asking questions, and promoting further study. This is new ground for many believers, so give yourself permission to make mistakes and learn and grow. After all, if you don't try it you can never learn by it, and your spiritual life and those who would have joined you in this adventure will be poorer instead of richer.

The group should be not larger than twelve and can be as small as two. Gather around a table, where there is easy access to Bibles, concordances, books and other study aids, and of course plenty of pens and paper. Keep some light refreshments available because once you get started you will be there a while ... believe me I know!

The Beit Midrash study can be likened to someone who steps off the dry land anywhere on the earth and into the water. The Bible says that one day "the glory of the Lord shall cover the earth as the waters cover the sea." Jesus said that those who believed in Him would have "rivers of living water flowing from their innermost being." From these and other Scriptures, we can see that God likens himself to water. As we study the natural so we can learn about the spiritual (1 Cor. 15:46).

All the rivers of the earth eventually flow into the sea, and all the waters of the sea are really one huge ocean, vast, deep and teaming with life. Sometimes the ocean is so incredibly calm and serene, at other times it is horrendously violent. There are paths in the sea, tides and currents that circle the earth. You can literally put a note in a bottle and throw it into the ocean at any place on the earth, and if that bottle catches the right currents it can go around the world. So it is with the Beit Midrash Bible study. You can start anywhere in the Word of God with a question or a comment; just step out into the vast ocean of God's spirit and be carried along to discover the "unsearchable riches of Messiah Jesus" (Ephesians 3:8).

Let me give you an example of how this works. A few years ago I was teaching a group of Bible school students in London about the Beit Midrash study. I had a group of them come forward for an impromptu experience of it. Their pastor and associate pastor joined in also. As the twelve of them sat in a circle in the front of the room, I asked them if any one had a question. After a few moments of silence a rather shy young lady raised her hand rather timidly. This by the way, is something you never do in a Beit Midrash study, you just speak out. The art of interrupting is very Jewish. The heated flow of discussion in the Beit Midrash study is such that interruptions become the normal, natural way for the flow, like the currents in an ocean, to proceed. What you have to learn to do is just interrupt the interruption and bring the discussion back to the direction you want it to go. The facilitator can use his authority here to guide the flow. As you can see the Beit Midrash study has its own rules of etiquette!

When I told the young lady not to raise her hand but just to speak out whatever was on her mind, she asked a simple but very profound question. "What is a calling?" In the traditional Bible study setting the question would have been directed to the leader, but here it is directed to the group. If you only ask one person, you only get one person's perspective. The Bible says that in the multitude of counselors there is wisdom. God will confirm things to you via more than one witness. So, I asked everyone to offer an answer.

Well, we stepped into the "waters" in London and the currents of the Holy Spirit took over. The anointing of the

Spirit began to move in people's hearts as new revelation and understanding began to emerge not just about "callings," but about a myriad of subjects. At one point the associate pastor literally jumped out of his seat yelling, "Hallelujah, praise the Lord, I just got an answer to something that I have been seeking from the Lord for a long time." He shared that it was a very personal matter and did not want to discuss it at that time.

This, by the way, is another very important element in the Beit Midrash study; we always respect each other's thoughts and feelings and never press anyone to share anything they do not want to. The Beit Midrash study is not about exposing anyone or making anyone feel uncomfortable. It is about creating a very positive environment for learning, discussing, investigating and growing.

He did share, though, that it had nothing to do with the initial topic that began our Beit Midrash study. The Lord used that merely as an entrance point into the waters of the Spirit, and the currents of God brought revelation to this man. God will use the Beit Midrash study as a means of bringing revelation to you.

The Beit Midrash operates according to some basic principles, which if applied consistently will make your experience very positive and spiritually enriching. The first and most basic principle is that of respect for your fellow students and their points of view. You must show respect in tone and attitude for each other. Respect does not mean agreement, but it does mean that you conduct yourself in a particular way that keeps the atmosphere free from opportunities for the enemy to come in and affect people's thoughts and feelings. We don't want to make people feel bad; we want to continually encourage more study. As I shared earlier, this is a place where we get some wonderfully difficult opportunities to grow into the image of Jesus. Showing respect for individuals, while disagreeing, even disagreeing vehemently (and this will happen!) with their opinion, is not easy. But the fruits of the Spirit can be cultivated fairly quickly through this type of spiritual experience.

A Beit Midrash study group can degenerate into a "Yes, we all believe the same thing and isn't that boring" home meeting fairly quickly if we alienate those whose points of view are different than our own. If we treat those who disagree with us in a disdainful manner they will not return to our study group and we will be the poorer for it. We have to learn how to learn from each other. Learning from one another is an aspect of the Hebraic model of the Church that has been lost to us. But God is restoring it!

God uses the natural world to reveal himself to us (Rom. 1:20). All throughout the natural world we see the constant theme of variety and diversity. God did not create one kind of flower or bird or fish or person. He created vastly different kinds. (Especially insects, have you ever looked at one of those bugs with a magnifying glass? They are seriously ugly! Whatever was God thinking when he created those things!)

The Scripture teaches us that the Body of Christ works like the human body. Our bodies are made up of organs and tissues and cells that are vastly different from each other in both structure and function. No one part of your body can say to another part of your body, "I don't like what you look like, or sound like, or what you do for the body so keep your 'stuff' away from me." Can you imagine what would happen to your index finger if it said to your liver, "Keep your liver 'stuff' away from me." Soon that finger would be dead!

Just as every part of your physical body needs every other part of your body, so we need what every other member of the Body of Messiah supplies for us (Eph. 4:16). We need people in our lives who think differently than we do. Different points of view, different interpretations of the Bible, and different applications, have to be examined, discussed and evaluated. With the right attitude and understanding, these different points of view can be sources of spiritual nourishment for each other. It is absolutely essential for spiritual growth that we have this diversity in our spiritual diet.

This is what the Beit Midrash can do for us. It can create an environment where the Word of God in all of its wonderful complexity can be investigated. Like the Bereans of Acts 17:11, we can come together to investigate the Word of God and the words of men *"to see if these things be so."*

The ancient rabbis expressed their comprehension of the realities of diversity of understanding, and the necessity for it, by analogizing it this way. They said that studying the Word of God was like having a group of students examining a huge diamond set in the middle of a table. As the light of the Lord came upon the diamond everyone from their own position and perspective saw different radiant and glorious colors. As they saw the magnificent colors and shared what they saw, they began to realize that what they were seeing was the manifold wisdom of God being revealed in part to everyone, and that together we get a full picture. No one individual has all of the wisdom or revelation.

While it is true that you may know more than anyone else at your study, remember what the apostle Paul wrote in 1 Cor. 13:9: each one only sees in part and knows in part. So no matter how much you know, all you know is a part. Every point of view is also many points of blindness. No one can see behind him, no one has eyes in the back of his head (no, not even your mother or sixth-grade teacher, even if they convinced you that they did!). We all need someone to see what is going on behind us. We need each other because we need each other's point of view.

Another analogy the Rabbis made that expressed the same understanding was the likening of the Word of God to a Rock, and studying it was equivalent to hitting it with a hammer. The small pieces that flew off the rock landed in the hands of those who were studying. Each student could examine their little piece with its own unique shape. They could arrogantly and ignorantly argue that their little piece was all there was to the rock, and that their little piece with its own particular shape was the shape of the entire rock. An absurd position, but it clearly illustrates the foolishness of so many Christians who adamantly hold on to their own little piece (their pet doctrines) and ignorantly proclaim that it is what the whole rock is like. Let us study the piece we have, and all the other pieces, so that we can all truly come to the *"fullness of Messiah"* (Ephesians 4:13).

When discussing divergent points of view, there will come a time when some passionate disagreements may be voiced. This is normal and actually very healthy. It means that people are really engaging the Word of God on a deep and meaningful level. Jesus said that it was passionate people who would lay hold of the Kingdom of God (Matt.11:12). Too many Christians, too much Church activity, and Church services in particular, lack any kind of passion. Far too much done in the name of Jesus is vapid, insipid and quite frankly booooring. The authentic ministry of the Holy Spirit is anything but boring. The Word of God is alive, active and powerful. It is like a fire, and when it ignites a human soul, that person will be full of the Zeal of God (Ps. 69:9 & John 2:17). God desires to ignite those fires in every one of His children. I believe that the Beit Midrash is a means that God uses to ignite those fires and to keep them burning.

A vital part of our Hebraic heritage that has been lost to the Church is the ability to, and the acceptability of, arguing the Scriptures. This was the common way for people to study the Word of God in the time of Jesus. When he was twelve he was seen doing exactly that with the elders in the Temple. Throughout His ministry Jesus was arguing the Scriptures with His adversaries and His disciples. The picture that comes to most of our minds when we read the word "argue" is a violent verbal display of emotion in which the arguers are very angry with each other. This is not the case here. To argue the Scriptures does not mean that you are angry with anyone, or they with you. It just means that you both have strong, passionate, feelings about your position. Nothing in this world is ever accomplished without passion. It is a missing ingredient in many lives. However, allowing your passion for your understanding of the Scriptures to make you angry with your brother or sister is sin. It opens the door for the devil to barrage your emotions with all kinds of negative influences. Bitterness and resentment will surely follow and will defile you and many others (Hebrews 12:15). The usual result is separation, disunity, mutual recrimination and vilification. The past and present history of the Church is replete with examples of this.

A Godly attitude of humility, coupled with an understanding that you only know in part, and that the part you know is incomplete, will help you mitigate against negative attitudes toward your brethren. Your own humility will say to you, "I could be wrong. Maybe I don't see all there is to see. Maybe there is some merit in what my brother is saying. After all I only know in part." Humility does not pray prayers that sound like "Lord, show them how wrong they are and how right we are." It does inspire prayers that sound like "Lord, show us all more of yourself and the truth of your Word."

In the movie "Yentle" there are many scenes depicting the students arguing the Scriptures very passionately. Although there could be great disagreement about the meaning or application of the text, there is never the accusation that someone is not a Jew because they didn't see the others point of view. Yet in the Church we are so quick to brand someone a heretic because they disagree with us. This kind of thinking is very destructive, because it robs us of opportunities to learn from each other. We must learn how to investigate God's Word with an attitude of humility if we are ever going to come to maturity.

Dealing with disagreements in a positive way is very important for personal spiritual growth, for attaining a greater knowledge of the Word of God and for building unity in the Church. A Beit Midrash study principle that is very helpful is this: When disagreements arise, record all of the points of view. Then have everyone in your study group investigate each one of them. (Do I smell homework?) After you have all completed this assignment, you bring together the results of your research and discuss the matter further. The issue is resolved when everyone is convinced in their own mind what the fruits of their own, and the others' study have revealed.

Apply the truths you have learned to your own life and allow yourself and others to observe the fruits of what you believe. Is your relationship with God increasing? Is your life bearing more fruit for the Kingdom? This, after all, is why we are studying the Word of God in the first place, isn't it? I have a personal conviction that if theology is not practical, it is not Godly. If it does not cause the fruits of the Spirit to be cultivated and manifested in our lives, then we risk being seduced by doctrines of demons that produce knowledge but no fruit, and lives focused on ourselves rather than on God, His Love and His purposes.

This strategy for dealing with disagreements leaves plenty of room for the Holy Spirit to bring more understanding and revelation into our lives. Instead of simply parroting what our ministers believe, we are impelled to study the issues for ourselves. The Beit Midrash study group agrees to temporarily set aside disagreement in hope that new information will be forthcoming to give us new insight and understanding. We must be open to whomever, or however, the Lord will choose to bring more truth to us. Moses taught in Deuteronomy 1:17 that we should not "recognize the face." The King James Version reads, *"Ye shall not respect persons in judgment, but ye shall hear the small as well as the great, ye shall not be afraid of the face of man, for the judgment is God's."* In other words, truth can come from anyone, even the mouths of babes. (Psalm 8:2)

I think another story from our Jewish heritage helps to illustrate the necessity and validity of arguing the Scriptures. There were two elderly rabbis who, whenever together, always argued with one another about the meaning and applications of the Scriptures. They spent many years doing this, until finally one of the old rabbis died. The other rabbi was so upset at the news of his friend's passing that his disciples asked him, "Rabbi, why are you so upset at the news of this man's death? All you ever did was argue with him." The Rabbi looked at his disciples and said to them, "You don't understand. Now I don't have anyone to argue with." These men were not angry at one another. They were sharpening stones for each other. They stimulated each other intellectually and spiritually. They enriched each other's lives.

We do more than agree to disagree—we go one step further. We agree that we only know in part, and that we should continue to study and pray for further revelation. Who knows who will be the vessel, or by what manner the Lord will bring us into more understanding. This attitude can make our walk with the Lord and with our brethren very exciting. You give God great opportunities to instruct you, and create very enriching spiritual relationships with brothers and sisters, when you conduct yourself in this manner. No longer are you at odds with your brethren over "doctrinal differences," but together you become fellow "explorers" and "investigators" of the Word and the Ways of the Lord. Unity can actually come out of diversity because you now see each other as a source of spiritual nutrition, exciting catalysts that provoke deeper study and greater insights into the Word of the Lord. Instead of satan getting the victory and causing separation, Jesus gets the victory and creates unity in His Body.

For too long the Body of Christ has done terrible damage to itself by trying to create unity based on agreement on doctrine or interpretations of the Scriptures. What we have done to the Body of our Lord is criminal. We are all guilty, either by association with, or misplaced loyalty to, a group and its progenitors, or directly by our own words and actions. Ranging from verbal assassination to outright murder, we have vilified, branded as heretics and apostates, and even martyred those who disagreed with our theology or our practices.

What we must do is search out ways to overcome this deeply entrenched historical demonic stronghold which has controlled and manipulated the Church for centuries. The prayer of Jesus for our unity (John 17:21) will be answered. I believe that part of the answer is the present-day work of the Holy Spirit in restoring to the Church this Hebraic model of Bible study, the Beit Midrash.

Chapter 6

The Hebraic Heart
of Leadership

The more we discover the true Hebraic nature of the Christian faith, the more we will be challenged to live according to the Scriptures. It is in those pages that we find the revelation of the Kingdom of God and God's invitation for everyone to enter into a personal relationship with the King and partake of the riches of His Kingdom. It is also here that we find the process by which the King trains, i.e. disciples, those who respond to this invitation. Only those who are disciples can partake of the riches of the Kingdom. Those who refuse this training never experience the reality of the Kingdom of God in their lives.

Central to this process of discipleship is the renewal of our minds and the reformation of our hearts. God teaches us how to think and feel as He does. In this way he determines whether He can depend on us to respond like Him, in word, thought and deed, as he entrusts us with more and more authority in His Kingdom. It is this process of learning to emulate God and be entrusted to oversee His kingdom that is at the heart of the Hebraic nature of our faith. The Hebraic faith revealed to us in the pages of Scripture centers on this theme. It is very different than all the other religions of the world. They are centered on manipulating the deity to serve the purposes of "self." The Hebraic heart is centered on personal transformation into the image of the Messiah and entrustment with greater responsibility in God's Kingdom.

The pages of Scripture paint a picture of our King and His Kingdom. They show us who he really is, and who we really are. They teach us the way to grow in relationship to him, to others, and even to ourselves. They reveal to us how the King wants His Kingdom to be administrated on the earth. Of central importance to that administration is the quality of its administrators, or using a more familiar Biblical term, its stewards. A steward is someone who is entrusted with responsibility and authority to care for another's possessions.

A leader in the Kingdom of God is simply a steward of that which has been entrusted to him by the King. If leaders in the Kingdom are not properly trained, motivated, and equipped, then the work of the Kingdom will be seriously compromised and its effectiveness greatly hindered. Leaders in this Kingdom are constantly being instructed and adjusted by the King to have a heart that reflects His own. As we seek the restoration of the Hebraic roots of our faith, we experience more and more impartation of these dynamics by the Holy Spirit. He is trying to give us a Hebraic heart, the heart of a servant who leads, and a leader who serves.

As we study the history of Christianity we can clearly see how those who were leaders in the Church became compromised in various aspects of their leadership. History testifies to how those compromises produced much ungodly fruit. Instead of building the Kingdom of God, compromised leaders built what I call the "empire of self."

Instead of surrendering all personal rights, goals, and desires to the authority of the King and allowing His interests to rule in their hearts, they allowed "self" and its interests to become the controlling influence of their lives.

Deceived by the subtleties of "self," they stopped being inspired and empowered by the Holy Spirit. As this deception deepened, the compromised leaders began to do things that protected their own "empires." People, money, and doctrines were manipulated and controlled so that they served the interests of each "emperor," rather than the purposes of the King of Kings.

The tragic result of this deception was the departure from our original Hebraic faith and the creation of a new non-Biblical religion that has generally taken on the title "Christianity." If we are honest, we can see that much of what has been historically called "Christianity" was, in fact, the formulation of a religion not based on the Bible and not built upon the Kingdom of God. As you study Church history, you will see how self-interest, though disguised in high sounding religious language, was at the heart of many decisions that bore ungodly fruit. The Biblical goal of making disciples (i.e. doing everything necessary to equip and mature believers) was eradicated by leaders who wanted to build their own empires. The deception was so insidious that this was all done in the name of Jesus and under the supposed authority of the Kingdom of God.

As the Church moved away from her Jewish roots, she grew further and further from the Kingdom of God. The Kingdom was replaced by the "empire of self" that grew into a political/military force. Using the power of the sword and the threat of eternal damnation, the corrupted Church subjugated individuals and nations, demanding their allegiance to her religious establishment. The Biblical picture of a spiritually empowering, organically relating community of believers that was lovingly ministering to and equipping people to fulfill their calling was virtually unheard of, and when heard of, was persecuted.

People were brought into an ecclesiastical system that did not create or nourish a personal relationship with God, or spiritually empower them. Nor did it want to. Its leaders sought to control and manipulate the people so that they could retain authority and power. They were spiritually compromised, and the fruit of that compromise was (and unfortunately still is today) people who themselves had (and still have) no real spiritual relationship with God and therefore no fruit of the Spirit in their own lives. Instead of building the Kingdom of God, they built (and are building) the "empire of self."

Throughout Church history, and today, we see leaders who have been compromised, to one degree or another, so that they were (or are) deceived into building their own religious empires. The subtlety of the deception is great, but the fruit is always the same: people are not given the spiritual environment they need to grow in their relationship with God and to fulfill their calling. They get trapped in a religious system that keeps them spiritually weak and dependent upon their "leaders" who lack a Kingdom vision.

The words and deeds of such leaders reveal the fact that they do not have a Hebraic heart, but a heart that seeks things other than the glory of the King and the spiritual maturity of His people. These leaders are locked into protecting and promoting their religious system because it gives them a degree of security and power. For others to grow spiritually is very threatening and resisted by various means.

Leaders in the Kingdom of God, however, are people who have been, and continue to be, impacted by the power of the Holy Spirit. The result of that encounter is a heart that seeks only the Glory of the King and the spiritual growth of those in His Kingdom. This kind of heart is exemplified and modeled for us by the Apostle Paul. The motivation of his heart is clearly seen in Colossians 1:28, where he wrote that he was doing everything he could to present every person complete in the Messiah. To present every person complete in the Messiah is the goal of everyone who is a true leader in the Kingdom of God.

If you are a leader, or aspire to be a leader in the Kingdom of God, and you have any other incentive or goal, you must carefully and rigorously examine the motives of your heart. Please understand that the deceptions that lead someone to build the "empire of self" instead of the Kingdom of God are extremely subtle. We are all so very easily influenced by the power and needs of "self." Diligent self-examination, open-faced humble prayer (i.e. prayer that entreats God to test you and reveal your own motives) and trusted Godly relationships are a few of the weapons we can use to keep the motivations of our hearts pure.

When His disciples came to Him asking about greatness, the Messiah explained to them one of the fundamental principles of leadership in His Kingdom. He said to them, *"The kings of the Gentiles lord it over them; and those who exercise authority over them call themselves benefactors. But you are not to be like that. Instead, the greatest among you should be like the youngest, and the one who rules like the one who serves"* (Luke 22:25-26). This theme is repeated in Matthew 20:24-28 when He said, *"You know that the rulers of the Gentiles lord it over them, and their high officials exercise authority over them. Not so with you. Instead, whoever wants to become great among you must be your*

servant, and whoever wants to be first must be your slave
—just as the Son of Man did not come to be served, but to
serve, and to give His life as a ransom for many.*"*

This is the fundamental motivation of the heart of a
leader that is revealed in our Hebraic religion. His is a heart
that is motivated to serve. It is a heart that only wants to
see the King glorified and to see His people come into the
completeness that He desires. It is a heart that is ready,
willing, and able to give its life for the purposes of God to
be established in others. It does not think about itself first,
it thinks about the King and His aspirations for His people.
Its only motivation is to be pleasing to the Lord and to see
Him glorified. It does not care what others may say or do. It
only cares about being faithful to the King and doing what
He desires in the lives of His children. It is always focused
on the will of God, not the desires of men.

Such a leader is willing to risk the rejection of people in
order to accomplish the purposes of God. Leaders with a
Hebraic heart are willing to suffer personal rejection because
they will not acquiesce to anyone's agenda. They firmly
resist being compromised by anyone or anything. They
will not commit spiritual treason by usurping or misusing
the delegated authority received from the King. They will
use that authority for building up the Body of Christ, not
for building their own religious empires.

Do not be deceived, people with corrupt motivations
can still exercise spiritual authority. *"The gifts and callings
of God are without repentance"* (Rom. 11:29). This is why
Jesus told us that on the day of Judgment many will come
to him declaring what they have done and He will order
them to depart (Mat. 7:21-23).

God's servants are not slaves, at the beck and call of
other people's self-centered demands. They seek only to

serve the purposes of God in other people's lives. They seek to disciple and equip the saints to fulfill God's will. Discipling and equipping others sometimes calls for uncomfortable confrontations and somber exhortations to repentance and godly living. Not only do leaders need the right motivation for serving, they need the right strategies to implement the purposes of God.

Discipling others is not easy. It requires much wisdom and spiritual maturity. These qualities are not obtained easily or cheaply. It is precisely because these qualities are purchased at great personal expense that we see so little of it. But God is raising up a new generation of leaders, a generation of leaders with a Hebraic heart, a heart to see the people of God become all that He desires.

When we begin to carefully examine the heart of a leader, we are confronted with the degree of sacrifice and servanthood the King demands of those who would lead in His Kingdom. We must look inwardly at our deepest motivations. If they are not purely Kingdom focused, then we need to earnestly pray that God will work in our hearts so that our motivations and desires would mirror His. We are all easily prone to allow our "self" to dictate our thoughts, feelings, decisions, and behavior. Because of this we must always guard our hearts.

Are you a leader in the Body of the Messiah? Do you aspire to leadership? Do you have a Hebraic heart? Are you willing to pay the price to be such a leader?

Chapter 7

Women in Ministry: Anointed for Service, Robbed of Opportunity

The position of women in ministry has for many centuries been troubling for much of the Church. As we go back to our Jewish roots, however, we discover that the true faith of Abraham provides both anointing and opportunity for women to fulfill their callings in the Kingdom of God.

As the Church departed from her Jewish roots, she lost her understanding of the Kingdom of God and adopted the pagan understanding of "gentile authority," which Jesus warned us against and prohibited His disciples from emulating. This kind of authority is by nature oppressive and repressive. It seeks to keep in power and authority those who by virtue of their military strength, political standing, or financial resources have acquired dominant positions in society. The Kingdom of God, as it is revealed in the Jewish Scriptures, is built upon an entirely different structure. The greatest in the Kingdom of God are those who serve (Mat. 23:11).

Those who are given authority in the Church are given it for the express purpose of serving the purposes of God in the lives of those in their care, never to manipulate them to serve their own selfish purposes (Col. 1:28). Anything that is not centered on the purposes of God in another's life is by definition centered on "self." Self-centered religion builds its own "empire" in opposition to the Kingdom of God. You can use this concept of a self-centered "empire" as opposed to a Christ-centered Kingdom as a very accurate measuring rod as you look at your own motivations, and seek to discern the motivations of modern Church leaders and those you read about in Church history. If traditional Church practices that have become the norm, and if theological interpretations of the Bible that justify those practices are selfishly motivated, then we must change those practices and the theologies that justify them. We are under a divine mandate to build God's Kingdom and not to protect that which sustains any other "empire."

Leaders in the Kingdom of God are vested with authority so that they can do what is necessary to help those committed to their charge become *"complete in the Messiah"* (Col. 1:28). All leaders who practice Biblical religion are anointed by God for one reason: to equip "the saints" for the work of service that they are called to (Eph. 4:11-16). "The saints" is a reference to all who believe in the Messiah, which obviously includes women. This means that all ministers are called to do whatever they can to help women fulfill their callings in the Lord, and not hinder them!

Before we look at the infamous "women keep silent in the Church" and "let women learn in silence" and "I suffer not a woman to neither teach nor to usurp authority over the man, but be in silence" verses, let's take a look at the big picture of how God sees and uses women in the building of

His Kingdom. It is when we see the whole story that we will understand what Paul was actually communicating. Then we will be able to see what God intends for His anointed daughters.

Let's begin by examining the Bible to see how God anointed women and then gave them opportunities to serve. These many examples are highly instructive for us as we seek to restore the Church to her proper Biblical foundations and women to their Biblical ministries. Please understand that when you read these small vignettes about women in the Bible, that we are not just talking about unique or special individuals but rather we are looking at them as spiritual types as they reflect what any woman can be or do if she will respond to the Lord as these women did. If we fail to see them in this way, their stories will have no power to affect our lives today, and the purposes of God in relating them to us in His Holy Scripture will be lost. They are *"examples to us who believe, upon whom the end of the ages has come"* (1 Cor. 10:11).

Consider:

Sarah, the wife of Abraham, is written about in the "hall of fame of faith" in Hebrews 11. There the writer says that *"Through faith Sarah received strength to conceive seed, and was delivered of a child when she was past age, because she judged him faithful who had promised."* How are you fairing today concerning the promises of God to you? Like this woman of God, do you judge God faithful to fulfill His promises to you, or do you judge him another way?

When **Rebecca** understood that it was God's will for her to go with a stranger to marry a stranger, she did not hesitate to fulfill God's will. When this woman of God was convinced about the will of God, she moved without delay, do you?

Consider the faith and wisdom of **Jochebed**, mother of Moses, Aaron, and Miriam. Committing her son to the small watertight ark she built, she planned for Pharaoh's daughter to find him and for Miriam to suggest that she nurse her own son. In this way she was led by the Spirit to be actively involved in the formative years of Moses' life, imparting to him the spiritual foundations for his future greatness. Could you do with your child what this woman of God did with hers?

Jochebed's godly influence is also seen in her daughter **Miriam's** life. The Prophet Micah mentions her as one of those God used to lead Israel during the Exodus (Micah 6:4). After the miraculous deliverance of Israel and the divine judgment upon Pharaoh's army at the Red Sea, Miriam, whom the Scripture specifically calls a "prophetess" became the first worship leader in Israel's history, singing and dancing with a tambourine, as she led the women in dancing and the nation in singing the praises of the Lord (Exodus 15:20-21).

Because of their boldness, wisdom, and faith in the goodness and righteousness of the Lord, **the five daughters of Zelophehad,** had the Law of God, the Torah, changed. God himself said that they "spoke right" when they insisted that women be included in the property rights inheritance laws (Numbers 27:1-9). Could they have been the first "lady lawyers" in the world? When you see unrighteousness do you have the boldness to confront it? These five women did!

Rahab, a woman of dubious character, (some rabbis call her merely an "innkeeper") also mentioned in the Hebrews 11 "hall of fame of faith," is a direct ancestor of David and Jesus. She had great faith, wisdom, discernment and courage. She was one who could "discern the signs of the times" and recognized that the formerly impregnable Jericho was about to be destroyed. Rahab's past life was no indication of her future success. When she came to faith, she obeyed and received her reward. What discernment about the signs of the times do you have? What are you doing about the things you discern? Would you take the risks that Rahab did? Would you have hidden spies?

Consider the wisdom of **Abigail,** and the desire for wisdom of the **Queen of Sheba,** or the **widow of Zarephath,** whose obedience to the word of the prophet Elijah brought supernatural provision to her home. What about **Hulda,** another prophetess, whom Josiah sought for wisdom and guidance when He found the Law of God, or the prayer passion of **Hannah,** whose intercession and future dedication and sacrifice brought to Israel the great judge and prophet Samuel.

Let us not fail to mention three of the most famous women in the Hebrew Scriptures: **Ruth, Esther and Deborah. Ruth** is the premier example of faith and devotion. Her plea to Naomi, *"Entreat me not to leave thee, or to return from following after thee: for whither thou goest, I will go; and where thou lodgest, I will lodge: thy people shall be my people, and thy God my God: Where thou diest, will I die, and there will I be buried: the Lord do so to me, and more also, if ought but death part thee and me,"* (Ruth 1:16-17) is one of the most famous portions of Scripture. Have you made the same commitment to the Lord?

Another famous quote is attributed to the beauty queen turned national savior and hero, **Esther.** When faced with the prospect of certain death for entering the King's throne room uninvited she proclaimed with faith and courage, *"I will go in unto the king, which is not according to the law: and if I perish, I perish"* (Esther 4:16).

Deborah was a prophetess, counselor, military leader, and judge. The Israelite general Barak knew the anointing of God that was upon her life and would not go out to battle unless Deborah consented to go with him. Like Esther, God used this woman to deliver the entire nation.

These examples of women in the Old Testament clearly show how the Lord anointed women and then gave them opportunities to serve His purposes. God never changes (Malachi 3:6). So why would He, or the apostle the Church claims to follow, now prohibit women from exercising their anointings or taking advantage of the opportunities God gives them? The answer of course is that neither He nor Paul has done that.

In the New Testament, we see women exercising their faith and giftings as God gives them opportunity. Consider these examples. The woman at the well was an evangelist (John 4:29-30). The woman with the issue of blood had faith enough to take the anointing right out of Jesus' body without Him directing it (Mark 5:30-34). There were three women at the cross (John 19:25,26), and two women at the tomb who were the first to see the resurrected Savior, and the first to proclaim the good news of His resurrection (Matt. 28:1, 10). There were women whose gospel preaching was persecuted by Saul (Acts 8:3,4) and Philip the evangelist had four daughters who were prophetesses (Acts 21:8-9).

There were Jewish women in the upper room (Acts 1:14, 2:4), and gentile women in Cornelius' home (Acts 10:24, 27,44) who received the baptism of the Holy Spirit (Joel 2:28,29), the purpose of which was to imbue the receivers with power to minister (Acts 1:8). *Why would God give women the power to minister and then deny them the opportunity to use it?* He wouldn't and didn't. But insecure, intimidated, and deceived misogynistic men would. In the pure apostolic first century Church women could exercise all the gifts of the spirit and did! In 1 Corinthians 11:5 Paul specifically acknowledges women praying and prophesying.

Women in the New Testament preached, prayed, and prophesied. In Romans 16:1 Phoebe is called, in the Greek text, a diakonos--a minister--of the Church. This is a masculine noun that is used in many places in the New Testament to describe individuals who do the work of the ministry: evangelizing, preaching, praying, and prophesying. we see Priscilla and Aquila, her husband, ministering together, teaching Apollos the Scriptures, overseeing a Church, and traveling with and helping Paul in the ministry (Acts 18:1-18, 26; Rom. 16:3; 1 Cor. 16:19). These are not things a woman who had to be silent could do! Junia, a woman, is called an apostle by Paul in Romans 16:7, and in Philippians 4:2-3 he mentions two women, Euodious and Syntyche, whom he describes as "fellow laborers in the gospel." How could you labor in the gospel and be silent?

It is obvious then that God fully intends for women to exercise all of the gifts and anointings that God imparts to them This being true, how could Paul tell women in 1 Corinthians 14:34-35 to be silent, and that it is not permitted for them to speak in Church? The answer is simply that he did not. He was only restating a quote in a letter sent to him about this and other issues (chapter 7:1). He responds to the quote by exclaiming in vs. 36; *"What? [are you talking about!] Came the word of God out from you? Or came it unto you only?"* Is it reasonable to think that he would stop in the middle of a chapter and contradict all that he had just written and was himself practicing?

It is not a shame for women to speak in Church, because he already instructed women to speak in Church. The whole content of this chapter is the balanced use of tongues and prophecy by both men and women. I believe that the difficulties that this text presents are cleared up when these verses are seen as a simple restatement of an issue posed to Paul by those yet bound by unscriptural Jewish traditions. These traditions (the oral "law" of vs. 34) kept women silent in synagogue and there were those who wanted these traditions to be carried over into the Church.

Did Paul really mean to instruct the Church that women are not allowed to teach in 1 Timothy 2:12? If he did, how could he expect them, as believers, to fulfill the great commission? Jesus told everybody to *"go into all the world and teach the nations…"* In like manner, those who prophesy do so that everyone can learn, the central goal of teaching (1Cor.14:31). We saw earlier that Paul encouraged women to prophesy. It is interesting to note that Jesus in His rebuke of Jezebel in the book of Revelation (2:20) did not censure her for teaching or prophesying, but for teaching and prophesying error. He could have easily taken advantage of that situation to end this controversy once and for all by saying, "Jezebel, you woman, be quiet! I don't allow women to teach or prophecy in my Church, you are supposed to be silent."

If women were never allowed to teach or prophesy, the elders in the Church at Thyatira would never have even allowed her to open her mouth. But because women were teaching and prophesying as a normal occurrence, she had the opportunity to speak. The Church was rebuked for allowing her to lead people astray, not for allowing her to teach. Indeed in verse 21 the Lord gave her time to repent of her immorality, not of her prophesying or teaching.

The immorality of Jezebel in Revelation 2 ties directly to our study of 1 Timothy 2:12. If you take the time to do an in-depth study of 1 Timothy 2:12, you will find that Paul was not telling women in general not to teach or have authority over men, but was in actuality dealing with Gnosticism and female Gnostic teachers who were mixing sexual immorality with Gnostic doctrines. The Greek word used in this passage of Scripture for "usurp authority" is *authentien*. This is the only place it is used in the New Testament. The normal word for authority is *exousia*. This rare verb had coarse sexual overtones. John Chrysostom's fourth century commentary on this verb uses the expression "sexual license." What Paul was actually doing was prohibiting female Gnostic teachers from mixing their strange doctrines and sexual immorality as a means of seducing the Church. This is exactly what Jesus was doing in Revelation 2:20-24. For a detailed treatment of this concept, let me refer you to Charles Trombley's book, *Who Said Women Can't Teach?*.

Throughout the Bible, we find women who had powerful personal revelations and ministries. Church history is full of misogynistic theologians and ministers who have, all too successfully, tried to minimize them as some special exception to the norm. But that is completely wrong and the Church has suffered tremendously because of it. One of the many doctrines of demons that the Church has believed is that women are inferior to men and that Paul meant to silence them and relegate them to lifetimes of spiritual imprisonment and fruitlessness. As we boldly confront those doctrines of demons, we will find ourselves in many intense spiritual battles. But the fruits of our victory will be well worth the fight. All the women in the Body of Christ will be set free to minister in the anointing of the Holy Spirit and take full advantage of all the wonderful opportunities God will give them to build His Kingdom. Satan knows how powerful women are in the Spirit and so he has tried to "silence" and minimize them. But as God restores His Church to her Jewish roots, those daughters of Abraham will be set free to do a great deal of damage to satan's kingdom. Amen!

God has one unchanging purpose in the earth and that is to disciple men *and women* who can inherit His Kingdom and be qualified to rule and reign with Him. By anointing His children with His Spirit and then giving them opportunities to serve, God is able to train such people. Let us now, as we begin the third Christian millennium, not hinder *anyone* from fulfilling God's purposes, but rather work together with Him to see *everyone* complete in the Messiah.

KINGDOM PERSPECTIVES
ON
YOUR JEWISH ROOTS

Chapter 8

Your Jewish Connection

O ne revelation to the early Church changed the history of the world: Gentiles could believe in the Jewish Messiah and receive the gift of the "Ruach ha Kodesh," (the Holy Spirit) without being circumcised or taking upon themselves the Law of Moses. In Ephesians 3:4-6, the Apostle Paul called this revelation the *"mystery of Messiah."* The New International version translates verse 6 this way: *"This mystery is that through the Gospel, the Gentiles are heirs together with Israel, members together of one body, and sharers together in the promise in Messiah Jesus."* Gentile believers in Messiah become co-heirs with Jewish believers and together become *"one new man"* (Eph. 2:15).

The divine creation of this "one new man," also known as the "ecclesia," the "called-out ones," or the *"Church which is His Body,"* (Eph. 1:22-23) has profound implications; particularly for its relationship with natural Israel. One significant question that demands a Scriptural and Spirit-led answer emerges: How should this "One New Man"—the

"Church"—the "Body of Christ" relate to natural Israel, which remains in unbelief concerning Jesus?

In order to answer this question, we must put aside any carnal feelings which are rooted in racial prejudice, and allow the Holy Spirit to cleanse our hearts so that we will be able to receive the engrafted Word of God. If we are unwilling to do that, God will pass us by, as He looks for those believers who will follow Him fully so that He can accomplish His purposes.

If the word "Jewish," or thoughts about the Jewish people causes a negative response in your heart, if there is a "theological" justification for your negative feelings, you must earnestly seek the Lord, and study the Bible, to receive HIS heart towards them. The demonic spirit of anti-Semitism is very powerful and must be rooted out ruthlessly. If it is allowed to have any influence in your heart or mind, it will prevent you from being part of God's end time purposes in the restoration of the Church's Biblical relationship and responsibility to the Jewish people.

Paul the Apostle had a number of significant truths to teach the Church about her relationship with natural Israel. In Ephesians 2:12 and 19, he taught that Gentile believers are *"no longer strangers and foreigners, but fellow citizens of the commonwealth of Israel with the saints."* In Romans 4:11 and 16, he taught Gentile believers that, through their faith in the Jewish Messiah, they could now claim Abraham, father of the Jewish nation, as their own father also. In Romans 11:17-24, Paul explained that Gentiles are now literally grafted into the Jewish nation, and therefore able to partake in the blessings that come from the rich root of Israel's *"Olive Tree."*

In Romans 8:15 and Galatians 4:6, Paul repeated the fact that the Holy Spirit within us cries out in the Hebrew language, the language of the Jews, that God is our *"Abba,"* which means "Daddy." This is the same expression Jesus Himself used in His hour of greatest spiritual need, when He cried out to His *"Abba"* in the garden of Gethsemane (Mark 14:36). God did not send His Spirit crying out in Greek, but in Hebrew. This is a point of no small significance.

Because believing Gentiles now have Abraham as their father in the faith, they enter into a family relationship with the God of the Jews and experience Him as their *"Abba."* From these verses we understand that Gentile believers become spiritual children of Abraham, the first "Jew." Because they also became citizens of the commonwealth of Israel, they are able to partake in the covenantal blessings promised to Abraham. By their faith in Israel's Messiah, they are able to *"share in the nourishing sap from the Olive Root"* and call the God of Israel their Father.

It is very important for the Church to understand that she does not replace natural Israel in God's plan. God has made promises to natural Israel which the Church does not inherit. For example natural Israel's covenant includes the land of Israel. The Church, as the grafted in part of natural Israel, should be involved in Israel's present struggle with the spirit of Islam to remove Israel from the land, but should understand that the land was never promised to the Church. The grafting of the *"wild olive branches"* into Israel's *"cultivated Olive Tree"* does not exclude the *"cut-off natural branches"* from the future purposes of God, for God is *"able to graft them in again"* (Rom. 11:23). It does, however, provide God with a platform to show the unbelieving natural branches the riches of His mercy and grace.

Gentiles, *"who were separate from Messiah, excluded from citizenship in Israel and foreigners to the covenants of*

the promise, without hope and without God in the world,"
(Eph. 2:12-13) are now by the Blood of Messiah brought
near. Gentile believers, by virtue of this grafting, should
now love the God of Israel, love the Jewish Scriptures
(all the books of the Bible were written by Jews with the
possible exception of that written by Luke), and love the
Jewish people into whom they have been grafted and from
whose roots they receive *"nourishing sap."* The Church is
called to demonstrate to the unbelieving natural branches
that their long-rejected Messiah is in fact the King whom
they must seek.

The life, love, faith, power and holiness of these grafted-
in formerly wild branches should be provoking the natural
branches to jealousy. This has always been God's plan. It
remains His plan. The question we must ask is, "Will the
Church in our generation rise up and fulfill it?"

The call of the Church to provoke Israel to jealousy is
one of the truths of the New Testament that has historically
been obscured due to ignorance or rejected because of
disobedience. Early in Church history, men of good
intentions, in their zeal to preach the Gospel, de-Judaized
their message in an attempt to make the Gospel more
palatable to Gentile audiences. In so doing, they opened
up themselves and the Church to "doctrines of demons."
This had the dual effect of separating the Church from her
place in the anointed roots of Israel's "Olive Tree," and
giving access to a spirit of arrogance toward the natural
branches that was in clear rebellion to the plain command
of the apostle Paul in Romans 11:18-21. The Church no
longer saw herself as part of the Jewish people, or as part
of God's plan to provoke Israel to jealousy. Instead she
grew into a counterfeit imperialistic theocracy which
lost its authentic spiritual testimony and the ability to
make genuine born-again disciples. Authentic spirituality,

based on an individual's personal relationship to God, was replaced by a human religious organization.

Instead of a living body of born again disciples growing into spiritual maturity, we see the development of a religion that created a hierarchical system of political, financial, and militaristic schemes that forced loyalty to a Church instead of promoting genuine spiritual growth. The true Church was tragically compromised. Once compromised, she came under the judgment of God for disobeying the apostolic command not to be arrogant toward the unbelieving natural branches (Rom. 11:22).

God's judgment for such arrogance was the removal of the life of faith from the Church. The historic evidence of this is seen in the above-mentioned steady decline and replacement of faith in the Church. This was in direct proportion to her rejection of the natural branches and her own inherent "Jewishness." The more the Church rejected her "Olive Tree" connection, the more she descended into institutionalized sacramentalism, spiritual darkness, and unbelief. As time went by, what began as a Messianic Jewish faith, based on the Scriptures and the power of God, became a thoroughly Gentilized Christianity based on political and militaristic power and Church traditions that were in many instances nothing more than a Christianized paganism.

All things Jewish were slowly rejected and in some circumstances actually forbidden. The Jewish people themselves were branded in such ways as to justify their persecution, suffering, and even death. This was a satanic strategy to keep the true Gospel away from the Jewish people, and thereby keep Jesus from returning, because prophecy states that Israel's re-grafting into its own "Olive Tree" is followed by the resurrection of the dead, which takes place when Jesus returns. (Rom. 11: 15)

The re-connecting of the Church to her Jewish Root system and to the Jewish people is of profound spiritual importance. This connection is in fact central to the eternal purposes of God for the entire human race. The second coming of Messiah hinges upon this connection. This is why satan so fiercely fights it. But what is this connection? How does it work? What does it look like? How can we enter into this connection and be part of re-establishing it in our Churches? In order to answer these questions we must ask some questions. The first one is, what does "Jewish" mean? What does it mean to be a "Jew?" Who is a "Jew?" The reason there are quotation marks around these words is that they mean different things to different people. They have become emotionally and spiritually loaded terms which can be easily misunderstood and misapplied. We must use the Biblical definition that God uses, so we all understand what God means when he uses these words.

The English word "Jew" is derived from the Hebrew word "Judah," or more accurately "Yahudah," which means "Yahveh be praised." Most authorities agree that "Yahveh" is the correct pronunciation of the Hebrew consonants YHVH, which are commonly (but incorrectly) pronounced Jehovah (There is no 'J' sound in Hebrew). This erroneous pronunciation is derived from placing the vowels from the Hebrew word Adonai (Lord) between the consonants of YHVH. "Jehovah" is the result. Yahveh is the word that God has chosen as His personal name forever (Exodus 3:15). To be identified with this name is to be identified with the God of Israel Himself. To be a praiser of Yahveh is to be a Jew. Those who are in a genuine, authentic, and life-altering relationship with Yahveh, who by virtue of that relationship live a life of praise and experience the power of that praise, are "Jews." That is, they are "Praisers of Yahveh."

In Romans chapter 2:28-29, Paul was declaring to the natural Jews that: *"..the real Jew is not merely Jewish outwardly: true circumcision is not only external and physical. On the contrary the real Jew is one inwardly, and true circumcision is of the heart, spiritual not literal; so that his praise (i.e. his Judaism) comes not from other people but from God"* (Jewish New Testament translation). When Gentiles come to faith in the Jewish Messiah, they are made part of the commonwealth of Israel. They receive the Spirit of Yahveh that cries out "Abba." They become the spiritual children of Abraham and are grafted into the cultivated "Olive Tree" that is believing Israel. Gentiles become spiritually connected to the Jewish people, as those whose "Judaism" is from God, not from men.

The Judaism they practice is that which is revealed in the New Covenant Scriptures for all who will repent of their sins, receive the Messiah into their hearts, and obey His commandments. The natural Jew, whose "Judaism" is yet outward, has not been "cast away," (Rom. 11:1-2), but is being kept by the promises of God for a future time of national re-grafting (Rom. 11:23). Beloved Gentile believer, do not make the mistake of thinking that your "New Covenant Judaism" has replaced the covenant promises that God has made with the natural Jew. You are called to see yourself as part of the Jewish people to complete the purposes of God. You are called to be able to provoke them to jealousy! Can you?

One major and grievous historical error of the Church is the belief that because they were now grafted into Israel's religion and adopted into this relationship of "Praise" through the Gospel, they were now the "true" Jews and had "replaced" the natural ones who remained in unbelief. The **truth** of God's plan to use grafted in wild branches to provoke the natural branches to spiritual jealousy was hidden by the doctrine of demons known as replacement theology. If, as this doctrine teaches, God was through with the Jew, and the Church is now the "true Israel of God" then there is no need to have anything to do with them let alone having to provoke them to jealousy. This document historically taught that the Jews were under the eternal judgment of God for their rejection of Jesus, and as such were to be punished as a witness to all the world of what would happen in eternity to all those who reject Jesus.

The fruit of this replacement doctrine has been horrendous. It actually promoted the sin of disobeying the apostolic command of Romans 11:18-22 to not be arrogant toward the Jewish people. This arrogance has produced centuries of horrendous spiritual darkness in the Church and the horribly sinful persecution of the Jewish people by the Church in the name of Jesus. In short, rather than a jealousy provoking testimony of the Gospel, this doctrine produced hatred—in the Church for the Jew, and in the Jew for the Church.

God's actual plan has never changed. He is simply waiting for our repentance and obedience. The plan is straightforward. *He wants to use the grafted-in wild branches to provoke the natural branches to spiritual jealousy* (Rom.11:11,14). The quality of the Church's spiritual life, the manifestation of the power and love of God (their 'Judaism of the Spirit' if you will) is to so shine that Jews will become envious, and be forced to reconsider the Messiahship of Jesus.

The challenge that the natural branches present to the Church is a very important reality for all 'spiritual Jews' (both Jewish and Gentile believers) to confront. Jewish unbelief demands that we prove, by the irrefutable evidence of our exemplary life of faith and love, that we really do have something worthy of their jealousy. The natural branches are used by God to make us examine ourselves, and our Churches. This system creates a "reality check" for all believers. It forces us to ask some hard questions. Do our lives emanate the love, joy, peace, and power that Jesus promises? Does our Church? If not, why? God is looking for a people who truly represent him in the earth. He is looking for His Church to be "true Jews," in "spirit and in truth" (John 4:23).

There are those who will argue that Jews will always find a reason to reject the truth about Jesus. This argument is based on the Jews historical frame of reference. They have usually only experienced hatred from the Church. A Church which seeks to "convert Jews to the gentile religion of Christianity," will never be able to provoke the Jews to faith in Jesus. However, a Church that sees itself as having been grafted into the Jewish "Olive Tree" and made part of God's Scriptural purposes for the blessing of the Jewish people, will act very differently to the natural branches than the way historic Gentile Christianity has.

When the Jewish people see genuine love and support coming from the Church, I believe they will be more and more open to listen to the testimony about their own Messiah. Love has the power to break down every barrier. When the Church begins to see herself as part of the Jewish nation, it will begin to love and support her properly. When that happens, wonderful doors of witness will begin to open for the true testimony of Jesus to come forth.

I recently heard a testimony which beautifully illustrates this point. A synagogue was badly vandalized and burned, and the local Churches rallied together to support the grief-stricken Jewish community. Money, political action, and physical help in rebuilding the synagogue poured in.

Actual acts of love and support demonstrated something to this Jewish community that tore down centuries-old walls of suspicion and mistrust. When asked why they were demonstrating their love for the Jewish people in this way, the Christian leaders simply explained that they knew about their connection to the Jewish nation: that the Jews really were their "spiritual cousins." They went on to explain that the Messiah had simply put into *their* hearts the love *He* felt for His natural brethren. One of the leaders of the Jewish community responded with these profound words, full of prophetic implications: "You are taking away my reasons for not believing."

Love can overcome any and all barriers. Love is the beginning of the Church's true testimony to the Jewish people. The barriers erected between Christian and Jew by centuries of persecution can be overcome as the adopted sons of Abraham begin to fulfill their call to love, support, and testify to their "spiritual cousins" in the Messiah.

Most Christians do not see themselves as having been grafted into God's new covenant with Israel. They have been taught that Jews and Gentiles who "come to Christ" are "converted to Christianity." The Gospel has been so "Gentilized" that its inherent "Jewishness" is virtually ignored and hidden. Because of the redirecting of the Church away from her Jewish roots, Gentiles who receive Israel's Messiah never hear that they are now part of the commonwealth of Israel and grafted into the "Olive Tree" of Israel. The teaching they have received all their lives omits almost all of their connections with the Jewish people. I believe that God wants to redirect Christians back to their Jewish roots so that they will begin to **think and feel** like "spiritual Jews" and citizens of Israel.

This issue of "feeling like a citizen of Israel" or even "feeling Jewish" is not an emotional plea for some romanticized response; but rather an expression of a work that I believe the Holy Spirit wants to do in the Church. God desires that the Church be fully reconciled to the Jewish people, so that she will be able to love, support, and properly testify to them of their Messiah. The first step in accomplishing this goal is for the Church to understand that she already is Biblically and spiritually connected to the Jewish people. Quite simply, the Blood of the Jewish Messiah, and His grafting her into the "Olive Tree" of Romans 11, has made the Church part of the Jewish nation.

As the Church begins to recognize her Jewish connection, she will again partake of a Jewish consciousness which flows from her spiritual roots. The Holy Spirit is moving around the world, causing Gentile believers to begin to feel their Jewish connection. *This is a supernatural work of the Lord!* Because of centuries of anti-Jewish doctrines, "Christian" persecution, and the resultant mutual animosity and distrust, there are huge spiritual barriers that have to be broken down. I believe the Spirit of God fully intends to break them down. The question is, will you be part of the reconciliation, or will you be left out? You can begin by praying and asking the Lord about the truth of your Jewish roots and allowing Him to make them real to you in any way that He desires.

Chapter 9

Israel, the Church
and the Return
of Jesus

The coming of Messiah is the great promise of the Bible in both the Old and New Testaments. For millennia, Jews have diligently prayed for the coming of their Messiah. For centuries, Christians have maintained their blessed hope of the return of Messiah Yeshua (Jesus). I believe that the Lord has shown me that there are four "reconciliations" that must take place before Jesus can return to establish His Messianic rule upon the earth. I also believe there now exists a unique window of opportunity for believers, as God's fellow workers (ICor.3:9, 2Cor.6:1), to labor with God in bringing four reconciliations to pass:

1. The reconciliation of the Church to her Jewish roots

2. The reconciliation of the Church to the Jewish people

3. The reconciliation of the Jewish people to their Messiah

4. The reconciliation of the Messiah to planet Earth.

According to Acts 3:21, the heavens must literally restrain the Lord Jesus until the "time of restoration of all things" that the prophets declared. As we study the writings of the ancient Hebrew prophets we find one major theme that is absolutely central to all their visions and prophecies. This is the constant and unwavering commitment of God to ultimately restore Israel to her land—and to "David" her King. David, Israel's greatest king, the one whose descendants were promised the throne (2Samuel 7:12-16), is the premier prophetic symbol of the Messianic King who is to come, and who will be the ultimate fulfillment of the promises of God to David.

"My servant David will be king over them, and they will all have one shepherd. They will follow my laws and be careful to keep my decrees. They will live in the land I gave to my servant Jacob, the land where your fathers lived. They and their children and their children's children will live there forever, and David my servant will be their prince forever" (Ezekiel 37:24-25).

DIABOLICAL DEVICES AGAINST ISRAEL

Upon hearing Peter's proclamation in Acts 3:21 that Jesus was being restrained in heaven until the words of the prophets were fulfilled, and knowing full well that the return of Jesus spells his doom, satan contrived a two-fold plan to prevent the return of Jesus. A study of Church history reveals this plan. The first part of the plan is seen in his attempts at preventing the words of the prophets from being fulfilled. Since the prophets spoke about the Jewish people ultimately being re-gathered to the land of Israel, he sought either to achieve the genocide of the entire

Jewish race, or force them to lose their national identity and distinctiveness by assimilation or conversion. In either case, if the Jews would cease to exist as a nation, the words of the prophets would fail to be fulfilled, and Jesus would be prevented from returning. But, God has spoken clearly that Israel would never be destroyed, or lose their national distinctiveness.

"Thus saith The Lord, who gives the sun for a light by day, and the ordinances of the moon and of the stars for a light by night, who stirs up the sea, so that the waves thereof roar; The Lord of hosts is His name: If these ordinances depart from before me, saith Lord, then the seed of Israel also shall cease from being a nation before me for ever. Thus saith The Lord: If heaven above can be measured, and the foundations of the earth searched out beneath, then will I also cast off all the seed of Israel for all that they have done, saith The Lord" (Jeremiah 31:35-27).

Satan, in his blind rage, believes that he can succeed in his attempts to kill the Jews or cause them to lose their national distinctiveness by conversion or assimilation, and that the Lord Jesus can be prevented from returning forever. This is why anti-Semitism is so widespread, and its manifestations so pervasive and deeply evil. Anti-Semitism is a demonic spirit that hates the Jewish people, not because they are Jewish, but because of their prophetic destiny in the fulfillment of God's eternal purposes. Anti-Semitism is a demonic spirit actually attempting to prevent the return of Messiah Jesus by destroying the Jewish people.

Hitler was not the first, and unfortunately will not be the last, instrument of satan to attempt the genocide of the Jewish people. The demonic spirit that inspires radical fundamentalist Islam is the same spirit that has tried to destroy the Jewish people throughout history. It has only changed its outward appearance; its goals remain the same: Kill the Jews so it can prevent the return of Jesus. No Jews, no fulfillment of Scripture, no fulfillment of Scripture, no return of Jesus.

In addition to this we hear Jesus make a very important declaration to the Jewish people in Matthew 23:39. *"...I say to you, from now on you will not see Me until you say, 'Blessed is He who comes in the name of the Lord!'"* They will not see Him again until (a very important word in the Scriptures, there are many things that will not happen until others things do happen) they say to Him "Blessed is He who comes in the name of the Lord."

In other words, Jesus will not return to reign upon the earth until the Jewish people call for Him to return. Please note that the "seeing" is preceded by the "saying." I believe this is the ultimate fulfillment of the pattern revealed to us in the book of Judges. At that time, whenever the Jewish people were facing potential destruction they called to the Lord who raised up a "deliverer" to save them. This is what will happen at the end of the age, when Israel, looking at certain destruction, calls upon Jesus to return and deliver them (Zechariah 12:9,10 & 14:1-5, Hosea 3:4-5, Deuteronomy 4:30).

Since the Lord Jesus must also wait for the Jews to call him back from heaven, we must consider God's plan for provoking such a response from a people who have been temporarily blinded to the spiritual truth that Jesus is the Messiah. As we study the Scriptures, we see that God has always intended to use the Church to provoke Israel to jealousy (see Deut. 32:21, Rom. 10:19, 11:11). Satan was also aware of this plan and launched his own counterattack to prevent it from succeeding. His work was subtle and very effective. By gaining entrance to the Church in her earliest stages, satan was able to divert her from the Scriptural pattern and distort her into a caricature of what she was called to be. However, we have, I believe, reached the point in history where Psalm 102:13-16 is being fulfilled, and satan's plan finally foiled.

GRECO-ROMAN INFLUENCES

As the Gospel spread to the Greco-Roman world, the influence of its philosophies and culture caused a gradual transformation of the Church. The Scriptures were effectively hidden from the common man, and the Church, instead of being a supernatural body of believers obeying its head in making disciples of the nations, became a military, political and religious hierarchical organization built around doctrines and practices that were shaped by a carnal desire for worldly power and authority. In essence a new non-Biblical (and therefore non-Jewish) religion emerged and took the place of the authentic Biblical Church.

Since satan was aware of God's plan to use the authentic Church to provoke Israel to jealousy and eventually to faith in her rejected Messiah (Rom. 11:11, 26), he cunningly used the influences of the Greco-Roman world to devise a strategy to distort, change, and corrupt the once Biblically-based Church into a non-Biblical organization that carried the name Church and proclaimed itself the worshippers and representatives of Jesus. The strategy of alienating the Church from her Jewish roots and from the Jewish people was successful. As a consequence, satan effectively accomplished three amazingly destructive goals:

1. He Brought God's Judgment on the Church

Satan was able to bring the Church under God's judgment for her disobedience to the apostolic injunction to not become arrogant and boastful against her own Jewish roots. God clearly warned of the consequences of such an attitude: He would cut the Church off (Rom. 11:18-22). As we study the history of the Church, we can see that this judgment truly was inflicted upon it. It is most interesting to note that the progressive loss of spirituality in the Church exactly paralleled the contemporaneous rejection of the Church's Jewish roots. The nourishment the roots provided was replaced with non-Biblical doctrines and practices that poisoned the Church. Instead of growing as a faith-filled, disciple nurturing, international community bearing the fruits of the Spirit, it descended into gross spiritual darkness where it remained until the time of reformation and renewal, when the light of revelation began to break satan's hold. This darkness is most clearly seen in the blood the Church shed. Instead of expressing the LOVE of God, which is the true testimony of a disciple of Jesus, the Church manifested the HATRED of the devil. This hatred, by the way, was not only expressed toward the Jews, but to anyone who dared to disagree with those who were in power at any particular time. Both Catholics and Protestants were guilty of persecuting those with whom they differed.

2. He Destroyed the Church's Relationship with the Jewish People

By effectively destroying the Church's relationship with the Jewish people, satan was able to prevent the Church from experiencing the "rich root of the Olive Tree" (Rom. 11:17) that the faith, history, Scriptures, traditions and heritage of the Jewish people provide. This "root-rejecting" Church made it virtually impossible for Jews to come to faith in Messiah Jesus and still maintain their Jewish identity. This has been a great tragedy because, firstly, had individual Jews had the opportunity to hear the true "Jewish" Gospel of their own Messiah, uncorrupted by Gentile traditions, untold numbers would have come to faith. Secondly, since Gentile believers had been grafted from a wild tree into the Jews' cultivated Olive Tree (Rom. 11:17, 24), the cultivated Tree's rich roots, heritage and background would have greatly enriched the lives of Gentile believers throughout history.

3. He Corrupted the Church

Because the judgment of God came upon the Church for her denial and rejection of Romans 11:11-32, satan was allowed access to the Church and was able to turn the Church into his agent of persecution and death rather than God's agent of power and witness. No one can deny the tragic, bloodstained history of the Church's systematic and unrelenting persecution of the Jewish people. By so perverting the Church and her mission, satan was able to virtually destroy the Church's testimony to the Jewish people of the Messiahship of Jesus of Nazareth. The Jews would never choose to believe in the "founder" of such a murderous religion, much less call upon Him to return from heaven. The words of Jesus in Matthew 23:39 would then never come to pass, and satan's plan to keep Jesus in heaven would succeed.

In short, as the "times of the Gentiles" draw to a close, God is restoring consciousness of her Jewish roots to the Church in order to achieve the second reconciliation: The reconciling of the Church to the Jewish people so that a jealousy-provoking testimony of the love and power of God can come from the Church to them.

More Than Academics

Mere academic understanding about the historical roots of the Christian Church, or "Jewish" flavorings for Church services, is not the reason for the Holy Spirit's move to restore the Jewish roots of the Christian faith. God wants the Church to return to its first century Jewish mindset, so that His Scriptural purposes for the Church can be accomplished. This mindset, reflected in the apostolic truths which had been lost to the Church through the centuries (such as the great overarching truth of the unity of the Church), are being recovered in many Churches, and are essential ingredients in the Church's restoration. Unless the Church once again becomes the powerful witness that she was at her birth, she will not be able to provoke Israel (or anyone else for that matter) to jealousy.

When the Apostle Paul wrote about his revelation of the Church (Eph. 2:11-22), he taught us that the Church was composed of Jews and Gentiles who were no longer separated by any walls of partition. The Church was, in fact, "one new man." He also went on to reveal that this "new man" was not only brought into fellowship with God, but also made a citizen in the commonwealth of Israel. This was a revelation complementary to Romans 11 concerning the Church's inheritance in, with, and among the Jewish people. (Please note how Paul uses the words "with" and "among" in Romans 11:17.)

Gentiles Must Be Grafted Into Israel

For too long, the Church has taught the Jewish people that they must be "converted" to the Gentile religion of Christianity, when the exact opposite is the truth. It is the Gentiles who have been, and must yet be, converted to a "Jewish" religion. Jesus of Nazareth is the Jewish Messiah, who sealed with His own Blood the New Covenant that was promised to the nation of Israel (Jeremiah 31:31). The book of Acts records how God opened the Jewish New Covenant, the true "Judaism of God," to all the Gentiles who would believe.

This true "Judaism of God" touches all areas of life. It gives us a view of heaven and instruction for successful living. The New Covenant Scriptures were written from a first-century Jewish perspective, not a second or third-century Greek or Roman perspective. We cannot allow those pagan societies to influence how we interpret the Scriptures or the realities of everyday life. Too many Church traditions have come under the influences of a Hellenic, rather than Biblical worldview, and the Church is still influenced by Greek and Roman philosophers, rather than by Jewish Prophets and Apostles. We must be restored to a Hebraic mindset that seeks to know God, not just know about Him.

Christians must more and more come to see themselves as "spiritual Jews." This simply means that when you became a believer in the Jewish Messiah Jesus, you were grafted into Israel's Olive Tree, made a partaker of the commonwealth of Israel and are considered by God to be "spiritually Jewish." This does not mean that you reject or renounce your natural culture or heritage, or that you have to copy modern day Jewish religious traditions or rituals. Nor does it mean that the Church has replaced Israel in the purposes of God. It means that spiritually you have joined yourself to the God of Israel and, like Ruth (1:16), have become one of His own people. My prayer is that, having this understanding, you would allow the Holy Spirit to show you the kind of relationships He wants you to have with your "spiritual cousins," the natural Jewish people.

In my spirit, I see a great move of the Holy Spirit in the Body of Christ, as authentic disciples reach out in love and support to the "natural branches" of God's Olive Tree (Rom. 11:17-20). I see the true testimony of the love and power of the Holy Spirit reaching out in many different ways to the Jewish people. My prayer is that such a testimony, about their long rejected Messiah, coming from a multi-national, multi-cultural, unified Church will so provoke the Jewish people to spiritual jealousy, that they will, without bias or prejudice, earnestly pray for revelation as they study the Scriptures for themselves, to see if the things prophesied about the Messiah are fulfilled in Jesus of Nazareth.

As the world turns more and more against Israel, I pray the Church will turn more and more toward her Jewish roots and to her Biblical relationship and responsibility to the Jewish people. As the birth pangs of the Messiah increase and Israel faces the moment of her greatest distress, I pray that the testimony she has received from the Church will inspire her to fulfill the Scripture that will usher in the return of the Lord. The Jewish people will finally call out to Jesus and say to HIM:

"BARUCH HA BA B'SHEM ADONAI"

"Blessed Is He Who Comes

In The Name of the Lord!"

Chapter 10

The One True Faith

If we are to accurately understand the Biblical relationship between the Church and the Jewish people and the real meaning and implications of the Jewish roots of the Christian faith, we must start with what the Bible teaches. We start with the Bible because that is where we read about the origins of the Jewish people. There we read about the revelations God gave about Himself, His purposes for them, and for all the nations of the earth. It is also in the pages of the Bible that we read about the origins of the Church and God's plans and purposes for the Church.

The Jewish apostle Jude wrote that believers were to "contend for the faith that was once delivered to the saints" (Jude 1:3). As we study the Bible we see that there is only one true faith in the earth, this "faith once delivered to the saints." It is this faith that was imparted to Abraham. It is this faith that was proclaimed to the people of Israel by the patriarchs, prophets, priests, and kings. It is this faith that was manifested in the ministry of the Messiah and demonstrated by the apostles. It is this faith that has changed people, nations, and history. It is this faith that is imparted to us when we repent of our sins and acknowledge that the God of Israel sent His only begotten son, the Messiah of

Israel, to die for our sins and rise from the dead, according to the Jewish Scriptures (1Cor. 15:1-3).

This testimony of the Jewish Messiah, which the New Testament calls the "gospel or Good News," is based on the prophetic revelation given by the God of Israel to the Jewish people through their prophets. These ancient Hebrew seers and oracles of God declared what the nature and ministry of the Messiah would be centuries before the actual events took place. They gave us a prophetic picture by which we could recognize the Messiah when He came. Speaking figuratively, symbolically, mystically, and literally, before the actual events took place, they gave us a "prophetic map" to guide us into the "one true faith," the faith of the God of Israel.

Once we understand that the one true faith for all people everywhere, in all generations is the faith of, and in, the God of Israel, we can move forward to understand the connection between the Church and the Jewish people. Jesus established the New Covenant or New Testament with the Jewish people in fulfillment of the prophecies spoken by the Hebrew prophets, most notably Jeremiah 31:31

"Behold, days are coming," declares the Lord, "when I will make a new covenant with the house of Israel and with the house of Judah, not like the covenant which I made with their fathers in the day I took them by the hand to bring them out of the land of Egypt, My covenant which they broke, although I was a husband to them," declares the Lord. "But this is the covenant which I will make with the house of Israel after those days," declares the Lord, "I will put My law within them, and on their heart I will write it; and I will be their God, and they shall be My people. And they shall not teach again, each man his neighbor and each man his brother, saying, 'Know the Lord' for they shall all

*know Me, from the least of them to the greatest of them,"
declares the Lord, "for I will forgive their iniquity, and their
sin I will remember no more."*

Jesus knew He was instituting a covenant with the
Jewish people that would allow Gentiles to become part
of the Commonwealth of Israel. He talked about "other
sheep" that would become part of the fold (John 10:16).
Many places in the old testament speak about the Gentiles
becoming part of God's people (see for example Genesis
12:3, & 22:18, Psalm 22:27, & 86:9, Isaiah 42:6, & 49:6, see
also Galatians 3:8). When gentiles actually began to come
to faith in the Jewish Messiah in Acts chapter 10, it was so
astounding in its implications, and so revolutionary in its
effect, that when Paul wrote the letter to the Church in
Ephesus he called this aspect of the revelation of the New
Covenant a *"... great mystery that was hidden for ages
past but now revealed to the prophets and apostles"* (Eph.
3:4-6).

A central aspect of Paul's ministry was the proclamation
of this revelation and the unveiling of the extent to which
the New Covenant actually went in providing redemption
for the whole world. What the ancient Hebrew prophets
predicted, and what the Messiah provided, is an opportunity
for people from all the nations of the world to partake in this
faith that was formerly only available to the Jews. This faith,
the faith of the God of Israel, the faith the Jews had received
at Mount Sinai when God confirmed His promise to their
patriarchs and made them a nation, was now available to
all the nations of the earth. This was all in fulfillment of the
promise God made to the patriarchs when He said to them,
"In your seed shall all the nations of the earth be blessed"
(Genesis 12:3, 22:18, 28:14).

As we study our Jewish roots we must be careful in our usage of particular words. We must avoid using those terms that have been re-defined by their common secular usage. We must also be aware that the devil is quite adept at redefining the meaning of particular words. We should use the words that God uses, and the definitions that He uses, in order to understand and to communicate clearly His truths.

One such word that is particularly powerful and often misunderstood is the word "religion." Our society uses this word in many different ways but it is often used as a substitute for the authentic Biblical "faith" that was delivered to the saints. Historically, and with tragic results, "religion" with all of its corrupt power politics and rationalizations, dogmas and philosophies, external trappings and traditions, has been substituted for the real "faith," with its power and ability to transform individuals, instruct nations, and change the course of history. Religious observance of outward forms and rituals has all too often been a substitute for inward realities. Religion lacks power to change lives, but Biblical faith - faith in the one true God - calls forth the power by which lives are changed. The Bible teaches that there is an authentic faith that God has given to the saints. Despite today's mentality of pluralism, there is in fact only "one true religion." It is the "faith once delivered to the saints" (Jude 1:3). It is faith in the God of Israel.

When we speak of the Jewish roots of the Christian faith we are NOT speaking of the present day Jewish religion, or Jewish traditions from centuries past. Although there is much valuable wisdom and knowledge available from these often extremely insightful rabbinical commentaries, we are referring to the "FAITH" that was imparted to our father Abraham, passed on to his descendants, imparted to the prophets, described and taught in the Bible, personalized in the Messiah, revealed to the disciples, manifest through the Apostles, and made available to you and me.

It is this "faith that was delivered to the saints." It is this faith that saves heals and delivers. It is this faith that transforms people and changes lives. It is this faith that empowers believers and overcomes the devil. It is this faith that healed blind Bartamaous and blinded the arrogant Rabbi from Tarsus so he could see the truth about Jesus. It is not religion, rituals, creeds, doctrines, traditions, buildings, hierarchies, or programs. It is the authentic personal revelation of God Himself, in, with, to, and through, anyone and everyone who will believe His Gospel, receive His Spirit, and obey His Word.

In the history of the Church's relationship with the Jewish people, a major mistake the Church has made has been its acceptance of the demonically-inspired doctrine known as replacement theology, which teaches that the Church has replaced Israel in the purposes of God. While the Church has been spiritually "grafted into" natural Israel, she is not a "new Israel" or a "spiritual Israel." These are confusing terms that mix concepts that are not the same. An apple is not an orange. A Jew is not a Gentile. A Gentile is not a Jew. The apostle Paul clearly says that there are three classes of people in the earth; Jews, Gentiles, and the Church of God (1 Corinthians 10:32). Jews are the natural descendants of Abraham, Isaac and Jacob. Gentiles are all other people. The Church is made up of Jews and Gentiles who by repentance and faith in Messiah Jesus have become partakers of the New Covenant. They have been spiritually regenerated by the renewing of the Holy Spirit, and have been transferred out of the kingdom of darkness into the Kingdom of God's dear Son (Colossians 1:13).

It is clearly Biblical to say that Gentiles become inwardly or spiritually "Jewish" when they come to faith in the Jewish Messiah. However, we must be clear in our understanding. When a Chinese person becomes a believer in the Jewish Messiah, he does not stop being Chinese. A Spaniard does not cease being Spanish, nor a Pole Polish, BUT any Gentile who comes to faith in the Messiah of Israel and receives the spirit of the God of Israel, who believes in the Jewish Scriptures, is grafted into the Olive Tree of Israel and receives its nourishing spiritual sap. He now has Abraham as his spiritual father, is adopted into the Commonwealth of Israel, and is a fellow citizen with the saints. (Gal. 3:14,29, Rom. 4:11-12, Eph. 2:12-13)

The authentic Church, therefore, is Gentiles and Jews who have been grafted into the spiritual life and power of the true faith of Israel. It is vitally important to remember that this "faith" is "Jewish," i.e. it came from the God of the Jews to the Jewish people, and through their Scriptures and Messiah, to the rest of the world. Jesus said, "Salvation is from the Jews" (John 4:22). The reason it is so vital to recognize the essential "Jewishness" of our faith is that this understanding provides the Church with the proper Biblical foundation for relating to the Jewish people. The Church must no longer, as it has done in the past, seek to usurp what rightfully belongs to the Jews, but rather seeks for ways to provoke the Jewish people to jealousy (Rom. 11:11,14). New historic steps in the purposes of God can be taken. The building of bridges of relationship between the "spiritual Jews" and the "natural Jews" has begun and must increase.

For centuries the Church's relationship to the Jews has been one of confusion at best, and hatred and persecution at worst. With the understanding that the Church has been joined to Israel and is sharing with her in the roots of the true faith, the Biblical relationship that God has always intended for the Church and the Jewish people to have can begin to bear His fruit. When the first century Jewish believers in the Messiah were cut off from the Jewish people by the edicts of the Jewish leadership, and conversely when, the Church's emerging Gentile leadership sought to cut the Church off from her Jewish roots, a tragically successful satanic strategy of hatred and persecution was launched.

The fruit of this demonic strategy has been centuries of spiritual darkness, for both the Church and the Jewish people. Not only did the Church fall headlong into centuries of spiritual darkness as the Apostle Paul warned would happen in Romans 11:18-22, but the Jewish people came under the influence of a system of religious teaching that was no longer based on the Scriptures, but on interpretations of Scripture by men who rejected the "true faith" made available through the Messiah. This double-edged satanic strategy had the dual effect of cutting both the Church and the Jewish people from the rich root of the Olive Tree. Both wandered in spiritual darkness and satan was able to keep each as an adversary of the other.

Today we are living in a time when God is restoring both the Church and the Jewish people to the rich root of the Olive Tree. Gentiles are rediscovering their rich heritage in their Jewish roots, and Jewish people are discovering their Messiah. As this discovery is taking place, believers the world over are praying for the Jewish people and the nation of Israel. They are seeking the Lord for His wisdom on how to testify to the Jewish people of the love, power, and reality of Messiah Jesus. The Holy Spirit is working among the Jewish people, revealing to them that their long-awaited Messiah is none other than the despised and rejected Jesus. There are more Jews believing in Jesus alive now than in any time in history, except perhaps during the first century. There now are more messianic congregations in the world than in any other time in history.

These are significant "signs of the times." God is moving by His Spirit to accomplish these things He spoke about so long ago. The Church is going to be restored to her Biblical relationship and responsibility to the Jewish people. The Jewish people are going to be restored to their Messiah, and Jesus is going to return to earth to rule and reign forever and ever, Amen!

Chapter 11

Jewish Roots and the Fruit of Love

For many Christians, the Jewish people and the Jewish roots of their faith are subjects that range from irrelevant to dangerous, or even heretical. Centuries of non-Biblical doctrines and actions have erected a barrier between the Church and the Jewish people.

This barrier can be thought of as a huge wall of thick, semi-transparent glass. Because only a small amount of light can pass through, vision on both sides is inevitably distorted. Imagine Christians are on one side, Jews on the other, viewing one another through the distorted glass. (This distortion can be compared to those non-Biblical doctrines and actions which affect the mental perceptions and heart attitudes of both sides.) Negative ideas, thoughts, and feelings begin to filter into the hearts of both Christians and Jews as they consider distorted views of one other, and how they are to relate to one other.

Through this distortion, Christians have historically come to see the Jewish people and/or the nation of Israel in ways contrary to Scripture: views best described as "tolerant" (i.e. "Let's just leave them alone"), or worse, "persecutorial" (i.e. "Kill the Jews!"). The root cause has been the spread of a doctrine of demons describing the Jews as "Christ-killers," and therefore "under the curse of God," and as a result "cast away."

A proper understanding of the plan of God as revealed in the Scriptures is necessary here. Such understanding always brings forth the Biblical fruit of love. Once this plan is understood, negative thoughts and feelings can be erased and replaced by the fruit that love bears. Seeing the Jewish people through the "clear glass" of the Scriptural plan of God will bring forth the fruits of love, support, and authentic testimony of the Messiah to the Jewish people.

God is looking for believers who will allow the "wall of distortion" to be torn down in their own life and replaced with a "bridge of relationship." The Church has a message, and a mandate to proclaim this message to all people, including the Jewish people (Matt. 28:19-20).

Historically, it has been the Church that has built the wall of distortion, despite the Scriptural mandate to be "ministers of reconciliation" (2Cor.5:18). It is therefore incumbent upon the Church, and not the Jewish people, to start the process of bridge-building. Christians must begin to actively tear down the wall of distortion and build this bridge of relationship.

Because the Church also has a mandate to proclaim the "Good News of the Messiah" to the Jewish people, we must be very careful to make sure that the message we are proclaiming is in fact the "faith that was once committed to the saints" (Jude 1:3), and make very sure that what we are proclaiming is the truth of God, and not religious or "Christian" tradition. If we are honest students of the Bible and Church history, we will see where much tradition has been added to the Scriptures, and where Church doctrines have supplanted the doctrines of "the faith." How can we effectively share with the Jewish people the good news about their own Messiah, and the New Covenant Judaism that He instituted, if our message to them is: "Convert to Gentile Christianity?" We must first understand where and how the Jewish message from the God of Israel about the Jewish Messiah - originally proclaimed by Jewish apostles and prophets - became "Gentile Christianity" that lost its inherent "Jewishness." As the Church departed from this "faith once delivered to the saints," (Jude 1:3) she lost her place as the "pillar and support of the truth" (1Tim. 3:15), because she began to proclaim a message no longer based on the revelation of the Hebrew Scriptures.

In place of this true revelation, an amalgam of doctrines and philosophies was propounded which formed a new religion in the earth. That religion has come to be known as "Christianity." To many, the Christian religion centers on services held in a "Church" building. There, an inherent separation between the "clergy" and the "laity" exists. The congregation observes a service, listens to a sermon, places a donation in the offering, and returns the next week for more of the same. This Christianity appears innocuous, even benign. Unfortunately, this appearance is deceptive. A closer examination reveals a "Church" history often rife with hatred and bloodshed.

As we turn our attention to the Jewish roots of the Christian faith, or, more accurately, the "faith of the Messiah," we place ourselves in a position where we can become open to discovering more and more about this true "faith once delivered to the saints." This is a challenging and exciting prospect because it places all of us in a position to reevaluate our beliefs and the "realities" of our faith as it affects our every day life. Learning about "our Jewish roots" will not spiritually profit us if what we learn is confined to academic concepts that adorn the doctrinal bookshelves of our minds. The truths we learn must be applied to our lives in practical ways. Only then will they deepen our personal walk and relationship with the Lord. This is the major reason for God's present emphasis on restoring an understanding of the Jewish roots of our faith. Another important reason is so that we, as representatives of the Kingdom of God, will be fully equipped and enabled to testify of the realities of Messiah Jesus to the Jewish people.

Before we can fully discuss our Jewish roots, we must understand truth. If the Church is going to be that "pillar and support of the truth" she is called to be, she must know the whole truth of her message. She must know why understanding the Jewish roots of her faith is important.

As we study the Scriptures, we find some interesting diagnostic tests the Lord has given us. We use these to examine ourselves to see that we are really in "the faith" (2Cor.13:5). The first, and perhaps most important, diagnostic test is the test of love.

Do our personal beliefs, Church doctrines, Scriptural interpretations, traditions and practices bear the fruits of love? Do they cause us to be more and more conformed to the image presented in 1Corinthians 13:1-8? *"If I speak in the tongues of men and of angels, but have not love, I am only a resounding gong or a clanging cymbal. If I have the gift of prophecy and can fathom all mysteries and all knowledge, and if I have a faith that can move mountains, but have not love, I am nothing. If I give all I possess to the poor and surrender my body to the flames, but have not love, I gain nothing. Love is patient, love is kind. It does not envy, it does not boast, it is not proud. It is not rude, it is not self-seeking, it is not easily angered, it keeps no record of wrongs. Love does not delight in evil but rejoices with the truth. It always protects, always trusts, always hopes, and always perseveres. Love never fails."*

Love is the hallmark of the Spirit of God. You cannot say that you have the Spirit of God within you if you do not manifest the fruit of love. The Apostle John wrote, *"Beloved, let us love one another for love is from God and everyone who loves is born of God and knows God. The one who does not love does not know God, for God is Love"* (1 John 4:7-8). Romans 8:29 teaches us that God is continually working with us to conform us more and more to the image of His Son. The image of Jesus to which we are being conformed is defined by the attributes of love described in 1Cor.13. Do our beliefs, doctrines, practices, and traditions cause our hearts to grow cold, or even become closed, toward others? Does our "religion" cause us to love more, or less? Does it give us spiritual justifications and rationalizations for compromises to our love, so that we feel justified in hardening our hearts toward those who interpret the Scriptures differently? The sobering fact is that individual believers, local Churches, and even denominations can permit their love for each other to grow cold because of doctrinal differences.

The Apostle Paul wrote in 1Cor.13:2 that "if you have all knowledge so that you understand all mysteries but have not love you are nothing." The Greek word for nothing here is 'oudeis,' the same word that Jesus used in Matthew 13 to describe someone who has "lost his saltiness" and is "good for nothing except to be thrown out and trampled underfoot by men." We must stop and consider the profound implications of this verse. The issue of love is central to "the faith once delivered to the saints." We cannot say that we are true believers or disciples of this "faith" if we are not moving and growing in love!

Please, dear reader, consider these thoughts. Is doctrinal correctness more important to you than your love? Has any kind of "spiritual smugness" crept in, causing your love for those who disagree with your doctrinal positions to grow cold? If the answer to these or similar questions the Holy Spirit may be asking you right now is "Yes," then be zealous and repent! (Rev. 3:19).

The Scriptures teach us to be *"zealous to preserve the unity of the Spirit until we come to the unity of the faith"* (Eph. 4:3 and 13). When Jesus returns and "opens up the Scriptures" (Luke 24:32) then, and only then, will we all share completely correct doctrine. Until then, our challenge is to allow the Holy Spirit to enlarge our hearts to bring forth more and more fruits of love in our lives (John 15:1-2, Gal. 5:22).

As we consider the Jewish roots of the Christian faith, we must remain keenly aware of the centrality of love to this "faith once delivered to the saints." When we move away from love, we are moving away from God, no matter how correct our doctrines may seem. The testimony of the Church is Love. The Biblical standard is Love. We must face the fact that if we do not have love we are not in "the faith."

As the Church returns to her Jewish roots, and allows the truths of the Bible to be her standard, she will find herself facing the issue of the Jewish people and the Church's failure to love them, even as she has failed to love her own. The issue of the Jewish roots of the Christian faith will force us to face this issue of love as well as many others. The way we respond to these issues will determine our faithfulness as servants of the Lord.

God has placed this emphasis on love because it is the realm in which He operates. Love is the atmosphere that allows God to manifest himself. Faith, which brings answers to prayer, works by love (Gal.5:6). Praise and worship, which brings the presence of God (Psa.22:3), is the fruit of our love for the Lord. Where Jesus is loved and where His love is allowed to flow, there He will manifest Himself. It is this manifestation of the Love and power of God that is at the heart of God's desire to restore the Church to her Jewish roots and to the Jewish people. God longs for the Jewish people to see the Church as He has called her to be: a worldwide community of redeemed people who love God, each other, and all men; a people who "know their God and do exploits" (Dan. 11:32), a community of faith and power in which the work of the Holy Spirit is commonplace.

Restoring the Church to her Jewish roots is but one step toward this glorious end. This is the step that takes us back to the Bible and the "faith once delivered to the saints." Discovering our Jewish roots takes us to a place where we can reexamine all of our doctrines and traditions, and rid ourselves of those which have come from men (or satan), and do not bear the fruit of Love. As the Church around the world becomes more and more conformed to her Biblical standard, and sees in the Scriptures God's strategy for her testimony to Israel, she can turn to the Jewish people and declare, "We are partaking in a Jewish faith. Your Messiah has filled us with His love. His power is demonstrated in our lives. Oh Israel, your Messiah is wonderful, come to Him."

Discovering our Jewish roots and understanding the Hebraic heritage of the Church is the first step in reorienting the Church to her Biblical relationship with the Jewish people. If the Lord Jesus cannot return to reign until the Jewish people call Him back (Matt. 23:39), and if the testimony that Jesus is the Messiah comes only from the Church, then the Church must regain a proper Biblical orientation and relationship to the Jewish people. She must repent of her past hatred and persecution of the Jewish people and begin to demonstrate the true faith from which she was originally birthed. We must understand that the overriding reality that will demonstrate to the Jewish people that Jesus is the Messiah is love toward them demonstrated by the Church.

At a Jewish believer's birthday celebration, an unsaved wealthy Jewish relative told her this, "My money has not brought me friends, but your faith has brought you people who love you." The love she observed caused an envy to rise up within her. She was provoked to jealousy (Rom.11:11,14).

May God so work in the whole Church of the Lord Jesus, that our love for each other and for the Jewish people will provoke them to jealousy.

Chapter 12

Re-placement
or
In-placement Theology

All over the world the Holy Spirit is stirring the hearts of Christians to discover the Jewish roots of their faith, and to understand the proper Biblical relationship that the Church is to have with the Jewish people. As this work of the Holy Spirit continues, we come face to face with various kinds of "theologies" and attitudes that seek to minimize the profound importance of this restoration. Some, unacquainted with Biblical truth, ignore or dismiss it as irrelevant to the everyday life of the believer. Others seek to prevent this restoration completely by proclaiming it a doctrine that historically has been used to keep the Church in an adversarial and persecutorial role toward the Jewish people. This doctrine has historically been known as "Replacement Theology."

Replacement Theology teaches that the Church has replaced the Jewish people in the purposes of God. It boldly declares that the Church is now the "new Israel," and that God has rejected and is punishing the Jewish people because of their rejection of Jesus Christ. Replacement theology teaches that there is no future for the Jewish people or the land of Israel. Through this doctrine, Christians are taught that God has finished His dealings with natural Israel (both the land and the people), and is now only concerned with the Church. Some Christians have been taught that the Jewish people and the nation of Israel are to be viewed as any other nation on the earth, having no Biblical or prophetic significance. At various times in history there have been those who called themselves "Christians" who taught that it was the responsibility of the Church to hate and persecute the Jews, as a testimony to the wrath of God that will fall on all who reject Christ.

Replacement Theology teaches that the Church is now to be thought of as the "new" or "spiritual" Israel. It claims that Christians have inherited all of the promises of blessing made to the Jewish people and to the land of Israel. The Church, as "spiritual Israel," has replaced natural Israel and is now the beneficiary of all that God promised the Jewish people. When the Bible speaks of God blessing the Jewish people, He really means the Gentile Church. When God speaks of blessing the land or the city of Jerusalem, He is actually speaking spiritually to the Church, because the Church is now the land or the city, or anyone or anything else for which there are promises of blessing. All too frequently, the theology goes on to teach that when God speaks of judgment instead of blessing, God is speaking to the Jewish people or the land of Israel. Never stated, but implied, is that the blessings are now reserved for the Church and the curses for the Jews.

An examination of history reveals that replacement theology has been the root cause of centuries of Christian persecution of the Jewish people. It has bred innumerable insidious doctrines which have manifested themselves in the worst kinds of hatred and evil. Jews were castigated as the most malevolent of men, forever cursed and continually to be punished for "killing Christ." The malignancy of this "doctrine of demons" (as the Apostle Paul appropriately named such perversions of Biblical truth) infected the Church with pride and arrogance. Ripped from her Biblical relationship to the Jewish people, and her responsibility to be a testimony of God's love, grace, and power, the Church was turned instead into a murderous, vicious, hateful persecutor of those to whom she was originally sent. How different history would have been had the Church discerned the spirit which propagated this great lie, and rejected it before it could have its disastrous effects.

Torn from the "rich roots" of the Olive Tree (Rom. 11:17), the Church descended into centuries of spiritual darkness. Hierarchical sacramentalism, imperialistic aspirations, and carnal power politics replaced the Bible's prescribed activity for the Church: making the nations disciples of the Kingdom of God.

The Church began to sweep pagans into her organizational web of sacramental rituals, using the power of the sword of steel rather than the Sword of the Spirit, as the legitimizer of her actions. No longer capable of imparting Biblical faith (the authentic, legitimate mission of the Church - preaching the Word of God, which creates faith in the heart of the hearer (Rom. 10:17)), she illicitly substituted humanly devised forms and rituals for the supernatural reality of the "new birth" (John 3:3,7 and 1Peter 1:23). Pagans were baptized, not because they had experienced a true spiritual rebirth, but because this became the price of admission into a politically and socially correct religion.

The Lord Jesus ceased to be the Head of the Church. The usurper, the devil himself, now became the illegitimate head of a perverted "Christian Church." Since satan was a murderer from the beginning, this "Church" did not give a second thought to shedding the blood of those who dared stand in her way. Not only did this grotesque perversion of the true Church murder Jews, but all who dared oppose its path to world domination, as *Foxe's Book of Martyrs* so grimly attests.

The once pure Church of Jesus Christ had mutated beyond recognition. The Church had become a murderer, manipulated by satan to accomplish his goals. The devil, knowing God's plan to use the Church to provoke Israel to jealousy, had succeeded in so distorting the "faith once delivered to the saints," that the Jewish people were only too glad to reject such an idol-worshipping, bloodstained abomination. "How could anything so evil and malignant come from the God of Israel?" they reasoned. "How could the "Jesus" they claim to believe in be our Messiah? Whatever he is, whoever he was, he is not the promised Messiah, for surely our Messiah could not, would not, inflame His followers with such hatred and evil."

The devil's plan had succeeded: a perverted Church was persecuting Jews in the name of Jesus. Jesus, the one the Jewish nation must believe in before He can return to destroy the devil. The Jewish people would now never come to faith in one whose supposed followers persecuted and killed them. A master stroke of evil genius.

But, ... God said in Psalm 102:13-16, that there would come an appointed time when He would arise and have mercy upon Zion, when His servants would feel pity for Zion's stones and compassion for her dust. This is the hour when God is arising. He is working in the hearts of believers all over the world. He is restoring the Church to the proper New Testament understanding of her "grafted-in" position.

He is restoring the Church to a recognition of her Jewish roots. He is stirring believers around the world to bring outpourings of love, support, and testimony to Israel. For the first time in history, the Jewish people will experience the "true Church," demonstrating the kind of love and power which will provoke them to faith.

The truth always brings freedom. The clear Biblical truth is that the Church has been "in-grafted" into relationship with Israel. The Church has not replaced Israel. Because satan saw the power that God would release by the creation of a new supernatural relationship between Jews and Gentiles, he has vigorously—and thus far successfully —opposed the fulfillment of this Biblical plan. In these days, God is restoring to the Church an understanding of this divine relationship. Gentile believers are understanding that they have been grafted into Israel's Olive Tree and are partaking of the rich root of the faith of the patriarchs.

In the realization that the Church is sharing this "root," new relationships and new dynamics of communication and understanding are able to take place. God has always intended that there be a flow of communication, testimony, and love between the "cultivated" and "wild" branches as a demonstration of His Kingdom. He will yet bring to pass such interactions and relationships. There is coming a day when the Church around the world will see and understand her proper relationship with the Jewish people, and will act to establish lines of communication and interplay. This is when the true testimony of Messiah will be demonstrated and understood. Jesus, who has been so maligned and misrepresented by the wiles of the devil, will be seen and understood for who He really is.

The reconciliation of the Church to her Jewish roots will result in the establishment of worldwide interaction between Christians and Jews. International dialogue will break down barriers of distortion and establish bridges of relationship. What God intended for the Church in the beginning will come to pass at the end. Gentile believers, the grafted-in wild branches, will be in a relationship with the Jewish people, free of religious and racial prejudice, where true dialogue and sharing can take place. Instead of Replacement Theology, there will be the creation of a new spiritual environment, where the true testimony of Jesus and the manifestation of the Holy Spirit can flourish. Instead of hatred and conflict, there can be love and dialogue. Instead of murder and mayhem, there can be mutually beneficial and fruitful harmony. Contrary to a satanically inspired history of persecution and death, there will arise a divinely inspired and empowered future filled with demonstration of the power and fruit of the Holy Spirit.

The ultimate fruit of Replacement Theology was manifested in the Holocaust. The spiritual roots of the Holocaust can be seen in the ways in which this demonic theology positioned the Church to take one of two basic positions in relation to the Jewish people: ignore them or persecute them. The truth is that the vast majority of the Church ignored the plight of the Jewish people, as the Nazi death machine sought to fulfill satan's plan to kill them all. Anti-Semitic attitudes continue today. Where is the outcry of the Church on behalf of national Israel? If the Church believes that the Bible promises the land to the Jews - if she believes that their regathering is part of the fulfillment of prophecy - why does she do so little to show her love and support?

While many Christians do not like the idea of Gentile believers calling themselves "spiritual Jews," I believe that this is an accurate appellation. For Jewish believers, the difficulty with this terminology is that the history of those who called themselves "spiritual Jews" has been one of "replace and persecute," not "in-graft and relate." For Gentile believers, the problem is a lack of true understanding, often coupled with anti-Semitism. In the past, those who called themselves "spiritual Jews" did so with the erroneous understanding that they were the "new" or "spiritual" Israel, God having rejected and replaced the natural Jewish people. This was the seed which produced nearly 1800 years of persecution, hatred, and death.

If only Christians had been rightly instructed that they were in fact "spiritual Jews," but in the true Biblical sense. They were grafted in alongside the natural branches, and should together have worshipped the God of Israel, partaken of the covenants, and enjoyed citizenship in the commonwealth of Israel. They would have understood that their position was given them by the Lord. They could have partaken of Israel's rich spiritual heritage and provoked the Jewish people to spiritual jealousy through their love and the supernatural demonstration of the gifts and fruits of the Holy Spirit.

God uses the concept of being "grafted in" to illustrate the close relationship that Gentile believers were to continually maintain with the Jewish people. This ongoing relationship was to be cultivated so that the Jewish people could receive a loving testimony to the truthfulness of the messianic claims of Jesus, as the Church demonstrated the love and the power of the Holy Spirit. Because the Church grew arrogant against the branches and was severed from the roots of faith, she was unable to maintain a testimony of the power of the Holy Spirit. The Holy Spirit's power began to wane in the Church, and the Church turned to false doctrines and traditions to justify its powerlessness. It is sad that today many denominations have the same "theological rationalizations" for their own lack of power.

As God restores believers to their Biblical relationship with the Jewish people, I believe that there will be a concurrent increase in the demonstration of the power of the Holy Spirit. God intends to provoke the Jewish people to spiritual jealousy and faith in Jesus by the demonstration of the love and power of the Holy Spirit in the Church. This is going to happen because it is God's plan and intention. To quote the ancient rabbis, "let us pray earnestly for this to happen speedily and in our days."

Chapter 13

Why Should My Church Study Her Jewish Roots? A Message For Pastors

There are many important reasons why Christians should learn about the Jewish roots of the Christian faith. But before we discuss them, let me address one common concern that many pastors rightfully have about this subject. When we talk about "Jewish roots," we are not teaching that Christians should come under the law of Moses, because "we are not under the law, but under grace." (Rom. 6:14) We are not teaching that Christians should appropriate modern Jewish worship traditions, such as wearing a prayer shawl (Tallit), or head covering (Kippah), or putting on phylacteries (Tiffillim). We are teaching the restoration of the authentic Biblical "faith once delivered to the saints" (Jude 1:3). This faith is the "Faith of Abraham," (Rom. 4:16) perfected and made available to the whole world by the birth, ministry, death, and resurrection of Jesus, the Jewish Messiah. Christian faith, as practiced in far too many places today, does not reflect Biblical Jewish heritage.

In many, if not most places, Christianity reflects the influences of non-Biblical belief systems, various human religious traditions, and worldly cultures. These influences effectively removed the Church from the "nourishing sap" of Israel's Olive Tree and allowed a mutation to non-Biblical expressions of Christianity. These influences have had the combined effect of diminishing or even deadening the spiritual life of the Church. The Christian world is full of Churches that only have a "form of Godliness, but deny the power thereof" (2Tim.3:5). Part of the restoration of the Church's Judaic heritage is the restoration of the power of the Holy Spirit in signs, wonders, and miracles.

All around the world, the Holy Spirit is moving upon believers to explore their historical Biblical Jewish roots to determine how God would have the Body of Messiah reclaim this inheritance. This reclamation includes studying (a very Jewish and Scriptural activity) the proper place of the Old Testament, including the Law, in our lives (1Tim. 2:15). After all, the same Apostle who wrote that "Messiah is the end of the Law for righteousness" (Rom. 10:4), also wrote that the Law is "... holy, spiritual and good." (Rom. 7:12, 14) He also testified that his "inner man delighted in the Law" (Rom. 7:22), and that its study has the ability to train believers in righteousness (2Tim. 3:16). It also includes understanding the proper place of the Feasts of the Lord (Lev.23) as appointed times for the Church to recognize the person, work, and ministry of the Messiah, which all the Feasts illustrate in powerful ways.

Not studying the redemptive significance of these Feasts has robbed the Church of important instruction. In like manner, not studying the patterns and principles of various spiritual subjects including worship, prayer, spiritual warfare, financial stewardship, community life and, one of the most important of all, how fathers are to care for and train their families, has seriously weakened the Body of Messiah for centuries. It is no wonder that the Jewish Apostle Paul wrote that the Hebrew Scriptures were "given by inspiration of God, and are profitable for doctrine, for reproof, for correction, for instruction in righteousness: That the man of God may be perfect, thoroughly furnished unto all good works" (2Tim. 3:16-17).

WHAT DOES "JEWISH" MEAN?

This "Abrahamic" faith was, and still is, essentially "Jewish." It is not Babylonian, Greco-Roman, European, African, Asian, or American. It was birthed by the God of Israel when He made a covenant with a Chaldean named Abram, and "converted" him to the Hebrew "Abraham." Abraham's grandson Jacob was subsequently "converted," and his name was changed to "Israel." As a result, Israel's descendants became known as "Israelites." God eventually established His covenant with the entire nation of Israelites through the Torah-giving ministry of Moses.

As history unfolded, the whole nation took on the name of the preeminent tribe from which their kings were drawn and their future Messiah would come: Judah. Israelites eventually became known as "Jews" (2Kings 16:6). The divine revelations recorded in the Old Testament give us the foundations of our "Messianic" (i.e. Christian) faith. These Hebrew Scriptures, in conjunction with the New Testament, also written by Jewish hands that were inspired by this same God, contain God's commandments and divine instructions for righteous human relationships and spiritual guidelines for establishing and maintaining a personal relationship with God Himself.

The divine influence of these "Jewish Scriptures" created a definitive culture and world view that was unique among all the nations and religions of the ancient world - because it was based on, and was the fruit of, recorded revelations of the God of Israel. We too should be converted, not only in our spiritual relationship with God, but from our former cultural and world views. Philosophies, traditions, or cultural dynamics which previously influenced us should be rejected when they are found to be contrary to the authority of the "Jewish" Scriptures. In Romans 11:18, the Apostle Paul makes this concept clear to Gentile believers in the Messiah: when anyone repents of their sins and receives Jesus as savior and Lord, they are grafted into Israel's Olive Tree and are made a partaker of the rich root of that "Jewish" tree. They are made "partakers of the promise" and become "fellow citizens of the commonwealth of Israel" (Eph. 2:19). Simply stated, Gentile Christians, by faith in Jesus the Messiah, have been grafted into a "Jewish" religion which has its own distinct spiritual realties, commandments, culture, and world view.

This "Faith" and "History"

This "faith" has undergone many permutations in its journey among the nations throughout history. It has been pummeled by politicians, mangled by mean-spirited theologians, stained with the blood of the martyrs, and renewed and revived by redeemed saints. Through all of this long history, the essential "Jewishness" of the faith has been generally obscured, purposefully hidden, and consistently vilified. I believe that this has been the well-defined strategy of the devil to accomplish two powerfully destructive ends.

First, satan wanted to create a non-Scriptural religion which he could influence and control. By removing the Church from the authority of the Scriptures, he was able to bring the Church under the judgment promised by God if she disobeyed the clear apostolic command of Romans

11:18-21, *"Do not be arrogant against the branches...you can be cut off also."* By successfully accomplishing this end, he was able to remove the engrafted wild branches from the anointed roots of Israel's Olive Tree. Once his strategy succeeded, the Church could easily be brought under the influence of numerous doctrines of demons. The history of evil in and through the Church attests to the success of this strategy.

Second, we see that the real goal the devil is seeking to accomplish is directly related to his first success. Corrupting the Church via these doctrines robbed the Church of her place in the anointed roots of Israel's Olive Tree. The result, as history so clearly testifies, is that the Church lost the demonstrative power of the Holy Spirit. This power was one of the crucial ingredients necessary to provoke Israel to jealousy. Paul himself told us that the *"Jews require a sign"* (1Cor. 1:22). Having no power to manifest such "signs," the Church has been unable to provoke the Jewish people to faith in Jesus as the Messiah. According to Romans 11:15, the dead cannot rise, nor the second coming of Jesus occur, until Israel comes to faith in Messiah. Satan's strategy is not only to rob the Church of her inheritance in the rich root of this Judaic heritage. It is intended to do nothing less than prevent the return of the Lord by stopping the Jewish people from coming to faith in Jesus.

HISTORICAL SEPARATION

As you study Church history you find that the Body of Messiah has been experiencing a slow but steady restoration of Biblical truths: the message of salvation by faith, the priesthood of all believers, the Bible as the sole authoritative source of doctrine, its translation into the language of the people, baptism by immersion upon the confession of faith, the restoration of the gifts of the Holy

Spirit, Church government based on anointing rather than institutional promotion, the restoration of all the equipping ministries of Ephesians 4, the commitment to fulfill the Great Commission, and many others.

These truths had to be restored because they were replaced by various "doctrines of demons" which had infiltrated and corrupted the Church throughout the centuries. I believe that a major reason for the restoration of the Church to her Jewish roots is so the Church can be restored to her Biblical relationship and responsibility to the Jewish people. The call upon the Church to provoke Israel to jealousy is one of the truths of the New Testament that has historically been almost totally rejected. In thinking that they had to make the Gospel more palatable to Gentile audiences, men of good intentions, misdirected in their zeal to preach the Gospel, de-Judaized their message, and in so doing opened themselves to the demonic doctrine of "Replacement Theology." This had the dual effect of separating the Church from her roots in Israel's Olive Tree and promoting a spirit of arrogance toward the Jewish people.

The Church no longer saw herself as part of the Jewish people or part of God's plan to provoke Israel to jealousy. Instead, she grew into a counterfeit imperialistic theocracy which lost its authentic spiritual testimony and the ability to make genuine born-again disciples. Authentic spirituality was replaced by a hierarchical system of political and militaristic schemes that forced "loyalty" to a "Church" instead of genuine spiritual rebirth and new life. The more the Church rejected her "Olive Tree connection," the more she descended into institutionalized sacramentalism, hierarchicalism, spiritual darkness, and unbelief. As time went by, what began as a Messianic Jewish faith based upon the Scriptures and the power of God, became a thoroughly

Gentilized "Christianity" based on political and militaristic power and Church traditions that were in many instances nothing more than "Christianized Paganism."

All things Jewish were slowly rejected and in some circumstances actually forbidden. The true Church was tragically compromised. I believe history shows that, once compromised, the Church came under the judgment of God for disobeying the apostolic command not to be arrogant toward the unbelieving natural branches. Unable to provoke the Jews to faith in Messiah, the devil inspired her to provoke the Jews to wrath, and further entrenched unbelief through centuries of malicious and incessant persecution. The Jewish people were accused of crimes and labeled in such ways as to justify their persecution, suffering, and even death. They were the innocent victims of hate-filled theologies which bred spiritual disaster for the Church and calamities for the natural sons of Abraham. This was a satanic strategy to keep the true Gospel away from the Jewish people, and thereby keep Jesus from returning—because prophecy states that Israel's re-grafting into its own Olive Tree is followed by the resurrection of the dead, which takes place when Jesus returns. (Rom. 11: 15)

PRACTICAL BENEFITS FOR YOUR CHURCH

By recognizing that we are practicing a "Jewish" faith as opposed to a traditional "Christian" one, we are freed from the historic, cultural, and demonic entanglements that have robbed Christians of their Scriptural inheritance for centuries. Whenever "tradition" stands in the way of renewal, revival, and authentic, disciple-empowering manifestations of the Holy Spirit, whenever the voice is heard that says, "we don't do that in our Church," with the implication that our Church has a more holy or sacred tradition, a "Jewish Root" orientation answers, "we are following the Scriptures and obeying the revelation of God, not the traditions of men, no matter how old or ingrained they are." After all, no Christian tradition is older than the Hebrew Scriptures.

This kind of thinking causes us to reassess every aspect of our Christian life, faith, and practice. Are we doing what we are doing in our Church or spiritual life because of our culture, traditions, or human philosophies? Is what we are doing according to the Word of God? Are we worshipping God the way He desires to be worshipped, the way the Scriptures teach He is to be worshipped? Or are we doing it the way we have been taught by our traditions, and in accordance with our own comfort levels? Are we in fact actually worshipping or merely having a "song service?" (Do we wonder why there is such a minimal presence of the Holy Spirit in most Churches?) Are we praying according to the spiritual principles of the Scriptures or according to our human understanding? How many Christians are frustrated in their prayer lives? Is it because they have never been taught to pray according to the Bible? So many Christians are victims of satanic strategies which have replaced the teachings of the Hebrew Scriptures with non-Scriptural traditions that the God of Israel neither respects, receives, nor responds to.

Let me reiterate that I am not saying Christians should adopt Jewish traditions or imitate the modern-day religious practices of the Jewish people. But a Jewish roots understanding demands a Scriptural basis for everything our Churches believe and practice. Not only will we be encouraged to study the Scriptures, but we will also be encouraged to understand how the Jewish people throughout history have understood them, and be freed to glean from them the riches of our own inheritance "among them" (Rom.11:17). This is something that satan desperately fears. He is terrified of the prospect of true believers entering into honest study of the Scriptures with the Jewish people. He knows the powerful witness of Messiah that will go forth and the great treasures that will be opened to the Church.

A Jewish roots orientation will cause the members of your Church to be more diligent when they read the Scriptures. It will create a healthy and mature attitude that says, "I want to know the truth ... not the traditions of men." As disciples of the Kingdom of God, they will be highly motivated to really dig into the Word and truly *"study to show themselves approved"* (2Tim.2:15). Paul wrote in 1Thessalonians 5:21 that we are to *"Test all things; hold fast that which is good."* The Bereans of Acts 17:11 are excellent models for the Church to follow. With so many winds of doctrine flying through the Church, we must follow their example and "make diligent study of the Scriptures to see if these things ... (about Jewish roots or any other teaching) ... be so." We must also make diligent study of history in order to identify the fruits of those doctrines and traditions we have accepted as truth. Many people will be very surprised to see the damage done to and through the Church when they make such a study.

Studying our Jewish roots will strengthen our families. We learn that God always intended for fathers to be the "priest" of their homes. The home, not the Church or the pastor, is to be the center of spiritual life and growth. The Church is to be an extended family, supplementing and augmenting the spiritual life of the home. Studying our Jewish roots will show us how the early Church, still firmly planted in those roots, conducted their "Church" services. They were focused on relationships and not on rituals, on families and not liturgies, on personal involvement, discipleship, maturity, not on theatrical type entertainment.

Many pastors ask, "Why is it important to say 'Jewish' instead of just 'Scriptural' or 'Spiritual'? Why is it necessary to continually put the word Jewish into our vocabulary?" It is important because of God's plan to use the Church to provoke natural Israel to spiritual jealousy. The Lord desires to restore to the Christian Church a mentality that causes her to be acutely conscious of the Scriptural fact that she has been grafted into a New Covenant made with the Jewish people, is believing in the God of Israel, is saved by, and waiting for the return of, the Jewish Messiah, and is trusting, believing and obeying the Jewish Scriptures.

With the restoration of this understanding, the Church can begin to pray and act in such a way that her relationship with the Jewish people and the nation of Israel will finally, after so many centuries, reflect what God intended from the beginning. God still intends to use the Church to provoke the Jewish people to faith in Jesus (Rom. 11:11). This will take a unified Church that can demonstrate the sacrificial love and miracle-working power of God. I wonder if we will be the generation that takes on the responsibility to bring unity to the Church, pray for the revival that will empower her, and allow the Holy Spirit to make us into the loving servants we are called to be.

A Jewish roots mentality also helps to create barriers that hinder demons from bringing their doctrines into the lives of your people. No worldview or philosophy—natural or spiritual—other than that which is according to the Scriptures is accepted. We learn how to study together, with tolerance and mutual respect, so that "iron"... really can "sharpen iron." We test our personal or corporate interpretations and applications of the Scriptures by examining the fruit they bear. Are they causing individuals to know and love God and neighbor in a greater way, and to manifest more fruit of the Spirit? If not, they are to be rejected. Jesus said, *"You shall know them* (both people and doctrines) *by their fruit."* (Matt. 12:33)

By studying the Jewish roots of the Christian faith, we gain a richer understanding of the God of Israel. We learn about His attributes, His nature, and His ways. We understand, for example, that the God of Israel is a God of history, and that history has a purpose. It is linear, not cyclical. It is moving to a predetermined goal. Because He has this historical view of life, we come to understand that each generation is connected, like links in a chain, to other generations. We therefore must, for example, deal with the sins of previous generations by acts of repentance and reconciliation. We gain insight into the plans and purposes of God, as we study, for example, His dealings with the Jewish people. One insight we gather is that the God of Israel is a Covenant keeping God, and that His promises, though they may seem to tarry, will come to pass.

We gain a greater understanding of the Bible that this God authored. By studying it the way the Author intended, we are brought into a dynamic, life-transforming relationship with this God. We are prevented from being deceived into following a god or religion that is constructed after our own imaginations, human traditions, or cultural preferences. We gain vital spiritual lessons that will mature our walk with God. We learn how to relate to Him as we study, for example, the various ways in which He has dealt redemptively with our many spiritual ancestors.

We gain a richer understanding of the person and ministry of Jesus, and the writing of the Jewish Rabbi and Apostle, Paul. We gain insight into the forms of worship and community life which the early Church practiced, as we understand how the Jewish believers brought their Old Testament faith, traditions, and practices into the Church.

We gain insight into how the early believers understood the practical dynamics of living out their faith in a hostile pagan world.

Studying our Jewish roots encourages us to study Church history and examine how and why the Church rejected the Apostle Paul's clear admonition in Romans 11:18, 20-21: *"Do not be arrogant toward the branches; but if you are arrogant, remember it is not you who supports the root, but the root supports you ... Do not be conceited, but fear; for if God did not spare the natural branches, He will not spare you, either."* This history study will have the healthy effect of prompting important questions about our faith and practice. Why do we do what we do? Have any of our Church doctrines or traditions nullified the power of God? What is the fruit of these doctrines and traditions? Are those who believe them and follow them really more like Messiah? Do our Church doctrines or traditions actually empower us to live more like Jesus, or do they rob us of our inheritance in Messiah? Are we more like the apostles in faith and practice? Or are we more like those who history teaches us departed from Scriptural truths?

Studying our Jewish roots will teach us how to read the Bible through Hebrew "glasses" and learn how to think Hebraically. In order to do that we have to take off the "glasses" of our own culture and worldview and put on those same "glasses" that Jesus and the apostles wore when they studied the Scriptures. It is a great spiritual adventure to learn how Jesus and the apostles understood the Bible. Understanding Hebraic thought opens up the Scriptures to us in life-changing ways. So many people are stymied when they read the Bible because they are reading it with a western, "systematic" mindset. The Scriptures are not systematic, proceeding logically from point "a" to point "b." They meander like a flowing river, where each bend is its own place of revelation and opportunity for increasing in intimacy with God. Remember, God is not interested in how much you know, but in how much you know Him!

Studying our Jewish roots will teach us that it is not enough to believe in Jesus—we must also learn how to be like Him. We will be confronted with some "things" which will make us uncomfortable: personal "things," doctrinal "things," traditional "things," and various other "things" in our lives and in our Churches. Being a disciple and being comfortable can be mutually exclusive; often, you cannot be both, and will be forced to make a choice. Learning to think Hebraically will confront us with the spiritual reality the Scriptures call the Kingdom of God. This Kingdom esteems very different "things" than the Kingdoms of this world. Studying the Bible as a disciple puts you in the place of training and changing, something many people do not want to do. Many want new information only for the sake of knowledge, or to impress others. God rejects such attitudes. He is looking for those who are willing to be changed into the image of His Son (Rom. 8:29).

God, who never changes, has given us a tremendous legacy in the Hebrew Scriptures. This legacy, and the ministry fruit it is intended to produce, is lost to us when we fail to study our Jewish roots. We lose opportunities to grow in intimacy with God. We also fail to develop the Biblical relationship with the Jewish people that God intends our Churches to have. The purposes of God are hindered for us as individuals, as Churches, and as ambassadors of the King.

KINGDOM PERSPECTIVES
ON
THE FEASTS OF THE LORD

Chapter 14

Living Lessons from the Passover Story

As is true of the entire Bible, the Passover story of the deliverance of Israel from Pharaoh's slavery and Egyptian bondage is filled with practical and spiritual lessons for our walk with the Lord, our battles with sin and satan, and our relationships with other believers joined with us in our adventure of faith.

To really grasp the importance of this story, we must understand the central place Passover holds, and how foundational it is, in the redemptive history God is unfolding as He deals with humanity. We must understand that the God of Israel is a God who oversees, controls, and redeems history. The historic events that God orchestrates, (i.e. those events that are working according to His redemptive purposes) are full of revelation about the nature of God's own person and His ways of fulfilling His own intentions. They are all part of God's plan of redemption that is continually unfolding.

Just as God is working in, and overseeing historical events in order to accomplish His purposes for humanity, so He is also crafting the events of our lives as individuals, to achieve His purposes for us personally. The favorite verse of so many believers, Romans 8:28, *"All things work together for good for those who love God and are called according to His purpose,"* is squarely based on the Biblical revelation that God is working out His plans in history to fulfill His ultimate intentions. Those ultimate intentions will be finally manifested when Jesus returns, you are glorified with Him and, *"The glory of the Lord covers all the earth as the waters cover the sea"* (Hab. 2:14).

As we study our Jewish roots, we gain greater understanding of the "ways of the Lord," and that those "ways," like the Lord Himself, never change. The way in which He dealt with ancient Israel is gives us insight and understanding into the way He deals with the modern Church. As we allow the Holy Spirit to re-graft us into those roots, we are more effectively able to partake of that authentic "faith once delivered to the saints." As authentic Biblical faith becomes more and more a personal reality, we experience our own individual multiple "Passover and Exodus," experiences as we are delivered from various false religious doctrines, systems, and traditions. Those non-Biblical beliefs and practices are like the gods of Egypt that seek to hold you in various kinds of spiritual, emotional, mental, psychological, relational, or financial bondages.

The Passover story reveals to us God's way of deliverance from bondage and oppression and His reasons for why He does it that way. The principles and patterns revealed in the original Passover never vary, as God effects all future deliverances from each and every kind of bondage you encounter. The apostle Paul understood how God, who never changes, laid out for us a "road map," showing us how He would fulfill His plans and purposes for our lives, if we would understand and obey the instructions available to us as we study God's dealings with ancient Israel (1Cor.10:11).

Before we look at some specific lessons, we must understand that there is one primary and fundamental reason for divine deliverance from bondage portrayed in the Passover story. God sought to set His people free from captivity for only one reason, so they could "worship Him" (Exodus 4:23). This is the most important issue for God in our lives. Jesus said, *"The Father is seeking for those who would worship Him in spirit and in truth."* (John 4:23) As we grow in our understanding, so that our worship is grounded in "truth" and in "spirit," we will have the kind of relationship with God that will allow Him to accomplish His purposes in our lives. He will continually set us free from every "Pharaoh" in our lives, so that we can constantly grow in intimacy with Him and fulfill the cry of Jesus' heart when He prayed for us that we would know the Father (John 17:3). A life of worship in "spirit and truth" is the foundation upon which all the other spiritual "building blocks" of our life can be built.

Let us look at the tremendously important and profoundly significant Passover narrative and see what lessons we can learn about the ways of the Lord for our lives today.

Israel entered into the land of Egypt when it was a place of sanctuary during a time of famine. God raised up Joseph (a type of Jesus), to be "savior" for them and open the door of safety and provision. In time, a new Pharaoh came to power "who knew not Joseph," and because of jealousy and insecurity brought the nation into slavery and bondage (Ex. 1:8-10).

Sometimes a good situation can turn bad. Don't despair! Learn the lesson of Passover. There is a season to enjoy the prosperity of a certain time and place. But if things change, don't give up hope or reject your faith. Learn the lesson of Passover. God never expects you to remain in bondage. He always provides a way of escape. Sometimes, because of weaknesses like insecurity, jealousy, pride, or greed, people change. They become someone you never knew before, or they act like someone who never knew you before. A new Pharaoh arose who "knew not Joseph." Again, learn the lesson of Passover. Cry out to God and He will, in His own time, send you deliverance. By whose hand it comes you may not know, but God will hear your cry.

God has His own time for effectuating your deliverance. You can try to escape by your own means or devices, but you will not arrive in God's appointed destination, the "Promised Land" of the fulfillment of His purposes for your life. You must wait for your time of deliverance and for the appointed deliverer to come. Moses could not be the deliverer God intended him to be until he was ready. God wanted to make sure that it would be His Passover that would fulfill His purposes, and not anyone else's. Your deliverer might be a person or it might be a particular set of circumstances, it might even be you. The point is, that the person or set of circumstances have to be made ready by God in order to accomplish His purposes.

As Israel's bondage grew worse—sometimes things get worse before they get better—they cried out to God. This is another important lesson. God responds to passionate cries for His deliverance and for His will to be done. God told Moses, from the midst of the burning bush, that "the cries of His people had come up to Him" (Exodus 3:7). (It is interesting to recognize just who was speaking out of the burning bush! See the chapter on the Angel of the Lord, p.183.) There is a tremendous power in passionate prayer. All through the Bible, and particularly in the ministry of the Messiah, we see how passionate people, and passionate prayers, moved God to action.

When Moses was ready, he had a life-changing revelation and was given a divine commission. Revelation always brings with it a commission. God always reveals Himself for a purpose. Everybody has a particular calling to fulfill, a mission to accomplish. Your assignment will probably sound to you like Moses' sounded to him, impossible. You will probably respond, or may already have, as Moses did, making excuses about your inabilities, weaknesses, and insecurities. God will then respond to you the way He did to Moses, *"I will be with you"* (Ex.3:12). If God gave you a mission to fulfill that you could do in your natural strength, you would not need God, and that wouldn't be much fun for God (which is actually an interesting way to think about it). God always calls us according to His purposes, which always have to do with building intimacy with Him. This, by the way, is the major difference between religion and Biblical faith. Biblical faith always stretches us and brings us into greater and greater levels of intimacy with God. Religion doesn't need God in a personal way. As a matter of fact, it prefers that God not get too involved, lest He disrupt our plans. He should only be there when we need Him to do something for us.

When God was ready, Moses appeared before Pharaoh. We are not told in the narrative how that was arranged. Pharaoh was arguably the most powerful man in the world at that time. No one could just walk in and talk to him, let alone demand that he set his slaves free! Don't you just love God's audacity! I believe the reason we are not told about how this meeting was arranged is because God doesn't necessarily tell you in advance how He is going to work out the details of your deliverance. The lesson is clear. Listen to what God says and leave the details to Him.

When Pharaoh refused to listen to Moses, God stepped in according to His promises. That which the Lord has promised you will come to pass. It might take suffering through some difficulties and a period of waiting, but the day will come when God rises up and says to the Pharaohs in your life ... "set them free so that they might worship me" (Ex. 5:1). It is very important to understand that at this point in the Passover story, the ten plagues that God sent upon Egypt were a direct assault upon the gods that the Egyptians worshipped. The God of Israel was showing Pharaoh and all the Egyptian people that He alone was God, as He sent judgment upon their gods.

The Plague of: Was showing God's victory over
1 Blood................................"Osiris"—god of the Nile River
2 Frogs.............................."Hekt"—rogs head goddess
3 Lice ...."Seb"—Earth god,
4 Swarming creatures ...."Scarabus"—Beetle god
5 Cattle dying ...."Apis"—Bull god
6 Boils.............................."Neit"—god of health
7 Hail.............................."Shu"—god of the atmosphere
8 Locusts ...."Serapia"—god of the Locusts
9 Darkness........................."Ra"—the sun god
10 Death of the first born ..."Pharaoh" and his son, whom the Egyptians believed to be incarnated deities

On the night of Israel's deliverance, God passed over the homes of everyone who had, in accordance with the commandment of God, placed blood upon the door-posts of their home. The blood was to be placed upon the lintel, the top of the doorway, and upon the door-posts. As the blood from the lintel dripped down to the floor, we see the outline of a cross upon the doorway. There was blood on the left post, on the right post, on the top, and on the bottom. The blood of the cross of the Messiah was pre-figured on this most awesome night. It was the blood that protected the home from the judgment of death. God already knew where the Jews lived. He had protected them from the nine previous plagues. But He wanted to see the blood of the lamb applied to the entranceway to their homes. It was the blood that protected them. The precious Blood of the Lamb of God, the Son of God, Jesus the Messiah, protects you and me today. I strongly encourage you to learn about the power of the Blood of Jesus.

From this display of power, we learn how God shows His victory over satan and all His emissaries, whom Pharaoh and the gods of Egypt represent. Satan might claim to control all the natural influences around you, and say to you that he has the money and the power, and try to put fear into your heart. The devil might say to you, as Pharaoh said to Moses, *"Who is the Lord that I should obey His voice and let you go?"* (Ex. 5:2). As we celebrate the Passover we are reminded how God answered Pharaoh: *"Against all the gods of Egypt will I execute judgment"* (Ex. 12:12). In the same manner God says to you, especially during this Passover season, "I will judge all the false gods that seek to control your life." As you seek the Lord in repentance, prayer and in the study of the Bible, the Holy Spirit will quicken His Word to you, and that Word will create faith in your heart (Rom.10:17). Stand upon the Word that God speaks to you. His word will never fail. Remember, *"all of the promises of God are yea and amen in Messiah Yeshua"* (2 Cor.1:20).

Chapter 15

Tabernacles:
Life from a Proper Perspective

The Festival of Tabernacles (Leviticus 23:39-43) speaks to us of the gathering together of the people of Israel to worship the Lord. They were to gather in temporary make-shift dwellings or booths called in Hebrew a Succot. These booths represented in the natural realm the temporary dwellings of the people of God as they made their way through the wilderness on the way to the Promised Land. This festival called the nation to gather in Jerusalem and spend a week living in these booths. This was intended to remind the people that their ancestors once dwelled in the wilderness in tents. They were to remember their past, so they would understand their present, and have a prophetic comprehension of their future.

God was insistent that they do this every year so that every generation would feel for one week what their ancestors felt like for forty years. God wanted them to have an actual experience of leaving the comfort of their own home and dwelling in these booths. This was to remind them of who they were, so they would understand who they are, and be conscious that God had called them to Himself for a future purpose. This is very important for us today as believers. So many people do not know who they really are because they tend to forget who they were and do not see themselves as God has called them to be. Because of this they are unsure of where they are going and live a life of spiritual instability.

Tabernacles serves a reminder of the great deliverance that God wrought in our lives when he brought us out of bondage to sin, and also of the transient nature of our life now. Spiritually we are all dwelling in booths. Our human body is only a temporary dwelling place. Tabernacles reminds us every year that we are not to take the wrong things too seriously because they are passing away, and we are also reminded to take the right things very seriously. This temporary dwelling, our time in mortality, is for the purpose of "Tabernacling" with God, to meet with God and to allow His purposes to work in our life.

If we only dwell where we are comfortable in the places of our own choosing, we can very easily stop pursuing the purposes of God in our lives and readily get caught up in the cares of this world. They grow in such importance to us that they consume our time, energy and talents. We can get caught up in the illusion that temporary things are really more important than they actually are. Tabernacles reminds us that this is not true. It shows us that life is temporary and that we should keep our priorities in order, that we should seek God's Kingdom and Righteousness first, because this life is as temporary as the booth is. Tabernacles serves to remind us that we should see all of life with its many problems, temptations, tests, and trials from this temporal perspective.

Another point of vital importance to us as members of the Body of Christ is that we are called to join with the rest of the Body in these booths. The picture we must see is the whole nation coming to Jerusalem to worship the Lord and dwell in booths. The Body of Christ is called to an understanding of the fact that together we are only dwelling in booths. We are to have eternity and God's eternal purposes in our minds and hearts as we relate to one another. We should not take earthly offences too seriously and allow them to hinder the fulfillment of God's purposes in our lives and thereby affect our eternal destinies. I think that there are too many believers who are not "dwelling in booths" with other members of the Body because of past hurts, offences, disappointments, and negative experiences.

Tabernacles reminds us every year that we are commanded by the Lord to come to His capital city to worship Him in these booths. We are called by the Lord to remember that our relationships in the Body of Christ are all about Him and His purposes. Our life is not about us, our happiness, our comfort or that which pleases us. You cannot dictate to the Lord who He can or cannot bring into your life. As a servant, and a disciple, you must allow the Lord to determine who you will, or will not, be in relationship with, and for how long.

As Tabernacles so clearly teaches, all relationships in the Body of Christ are for a season. Indeed, Tabernacles reminds us of the temporary nature of all aspects of this life. We must have this understanding and a heart for the purposes of God, so that we can say to the Lord and to ourselves, that those relationships that are not particularly comfortable have a purpose. God has caused us to dwell together, He has caused us to "Tabernacle" together. So let us "Tabernacle" with the Lord and with each other to find out the lesson God wants us to learn. Seasons can be of varied durations, but they are merely seasons. So rejoice in that, let Tabernacles instruct you. Do not be overly concerned; just ask God what He wants you to learn from this time of sharing the "Tabernacle" together.

Relax! Tabernacles is just one of the ways God reminds us that we have been invited to worship Him and to enjoy fellowship with Him. God is searching for us to enter into a deeper relationship with Him. He wants us to "Tabernacle" with Him, that is why Jesus came to "Tabernacle" with us. (John 1: 14)

It is very difficult to worry when you are truly worshiping God. When the anointing of the Spirit comes down, as it always does when we are truly worshiping the Lord, His sweet loving presence always speaks peace into our hearts. It lets us know everything will be OK, that "All things will work together for good ..." (Rom. 8:28). So relax, enjoy this season, and let it remind you to enjoy your life "Tabernacling" with God.

Chapter 16

Shavuot: Presenting Ourselves for Transformation

As with all the appointed Feasts set forth by the Lord in His sacred calendar, the festival of Shavuot portrays an important part of God's plan for empowering us to experience the realities of His Kingdom. Shavuot commemorates, in the natural realm, the beginning of the spring harvest and in the Spiritual realm, the beginning of our transformation. Passover, which precedes Shavuot by 50 days (hence the Greek name 'Pentecost'), signifies the shedding of the Messiah's blood so that death would "Passover" us and we would be delivered from the power of sin and satan. Shavuot signifies the presentation of our lives to God as His children, ready to be trained as heirs to share the throne with the King. (2Tim 2:12, Rev 5:10, 20:6, 22:5).

On Shavuot the high priest waved two loaves of bread, baked with leaven, before the Lord (Lev. 23:17). The fact that they had leaven in them is central to our understanding of the spiritual application of this feast. Unleavened bread (matzo) is the central symbol of the Passover representing the Messiah's sinless life. The first loaves of bread that are produced by the harvest have leaven, symbolizing our sin-infected humanity. God does not reject us because our human nature is yet imperfect. He only asks that we present it to Him. This small but tremendously important fact is often overlooked by many believers, with much spiritual devastation as a result. Indeed many stop walking with the Lord because they became preoccupied with their own "humanity" with its predisposition to sin. They get discouraged and defeated, as they become disgusted with their own continual failures. Eventually condemnation sets in as they allow themselves to think like this: "I can't live as a Christian. It's too hard. I keep falling into sin. Why bother, it's hopeless."

This is a great tragedy because as Shavuot teaches us, we are to continually present ourselves, with our sinful nature, to the Lord. Then He is able to continue His great work of redemption and reformation in our lives. The Jewish apostle Paul, expressed this fundamental truth of the Torah as he continually exhorted the Messiah's disciples to "present themselves" to the Lord (Rom. 8:16-19, 12:1, 2Tim 2:15). God set up the festival of Shavuot as an annual convocation for the nation of Israel to observe. It is insightful to know that one of the meanings of the Hebrew word for convocation is "rehearsal." We are to be rehearsing, i.e., continually practicing, these spiritual "exercises" until they become experiential realities in our lives. The fact that God wants us to continually "rehearse" these truths shows us very clearly the fatherly heart of God. He continually desires to receive us as His beloved children (Matt. 11:28-30). He longs to transform us, so we can be qualified to rule and reign with him over all of creation (2Tim. 2:12, Rom 8:29, 2Cor. 3:18).

Understanding that we are "students" in the process of being transformed and trained to rule and reign with

God gives us an eternal perspective on all our trials and tribulations, as well as our continual proclivity to sin. This understanding and perspective is essential for our life as a disciple. This perspective enables us to maintain a healthy, vibrant, and growing relationship with God. It enables us to interpret the circumstances and situations of our life according to God's wisdom and revelation. This "eternal perspective" creates a spiritual, emotional, and psychological space in our lives for God to do His transformational work in us. Without this perspective and understanding, we will be left to our own abilities to understand, explain, ignore or deny the experiences of our life. We become mere survivors simply enduring life, rather than overcomers who are thriving or "reigning in life," which Paul says is our inheritance in the Messiah (Rom. 5:17). This perspective and understanding opens our lives to an exciting, ever-expanding relationship with God. Prayer becomes a vital, integral part of our everyday existence. We desire to be in constant communication with heaven because we need the wisdom and power of God to be good students in His school. We need help with our "lessons" and power to allow the changes He wants to make in our lives.

Without this perspective, it is very easy for the "leaven" in our lives to harden our hearts toward God and others. Without this perspective, condemnation can easily overtake us. We can become convinced that we will never "make it," and so we "backslide" and give up walking with the Lord. Without this perspective, sin will get an advantage over us. Sin is spoken of in many different ways in the Bible. In Hebrews 3:13, it is spoken of as being deceitful. This means that it is very subtle in its ability to corrupt our thoughts and feelings and to distort and then destroy our relationship with God and other people. The leaven in our lives, if left unpresented to God, will harden our hearts as surely as bread left uneaten will get as hard as a rock.

When we remember the lesson of Shavuot, that we are commanded to continually present ourselves with our "leaven," to God, we are able to keep our perspective. We can continually maintain direction, and ultimately complete our training. Then on that great day we will hear the Lord say to us these awesome words: *"Well done, my good and faithful servant: you have been faithful over a few things, I will make you ruler over many things: enter into the joy of your Lord"* (Mat 25:21).

It is precisely because this is what the Father desires to say to us that the Messiah told His disciples to wait for Shavuot when they would receive the great gift of the Father, the Holy Spirit. The Holy Spirit was to come with a very special purpose. His job would be to comfort, guide, teach, and empower and transform all those who would come to faith in the Messiah and follow Him as one of His "students" (John 14:26, Acts, 1:8, 9:31, Rom. 5:5, Rom. 15:13, Titus 3:5). When we come to the Lord with the attitude of a "student," everything in our life changes. It makes a tremendous change in our thinking. Instead of condemning ourselves, or allowing other people or demonic spirits to condemn us, we simply look at each situation with the attitude that says, "The King invited me, with all of my "leaven" into His Kingdom, and now I am a student in His Kingdom. I am continually learning how to walk with, and obey, the King. He is not condemning me. He knows my weaknesses and my limitations. He Himself has experienced all of our human weaknesses, and He continually encourages me to be faithful as I learn, change and grow."

Because I desire to grow in every way the Lord wants me to, each day I repent. Every day I turn to the Lord and say: "Your mercies are new each morning, so now I present myself as your student for my teacher, the Holy Spirit, to comfort me, teach me, and transform me into Your image" (Rom. 8:29, Col. 3:10). We do not turn away from God and allow the deceitfulness of sin to harden our hearts. We remain faithful students in His "School of the Spirit." We continue to show up for our "classes," where our great teacher, comforter, and guide can do His supernatural work in our lives.

Too many believers do not know how to receive the ministry of the Holy Spirit. When we read of Him being our teacher and comforter, we usually remember our experiences with the teachers we had in school. Few of us had teachers who would "comfort" us when we made mistakes learning something new, but those of us who did have such teachers, never forget them. They created a psychological, emotional, and intellectual environment encouraging our growth. They did not condemn us, but encouraged us. They strengthened our resolve to overcome our difficulties. They were there to guide us step by step through the learning process.

School with such teachers was fun! It was fun because learning was created by God to be pleasurable and joyful. Today scientists have discovered that when we learn new things, our brains produce endorphins, which are pleasure producing chemicals. God has created us biologically to love learning. When learning is not joyful, because our teachers are not "comforters," not only don't we learn, we even hate to go to school. It becomes a place of pain and frustration. This is why many people no longer walk with the Lord, no longer go to Church, or have any Christian fellowship. They never learned how to let the Holy Spirit be their comforter as they walk through the difficulties of life.

Some believers have made the common mistake of putting leaders in the place of the Holy Spirit. They wrongly think that what their leaders do, or do not do, is what the Holy Spirit is doing or not doing. When those leaders fail (as they inevitably will), it is easy to get disgusted, disappointed, discouraged, and depressed. Anyone can fall prey to the error of looking to people rather than looking to God. They think like this: "Well, if God is like that, I want nothing to do with Him." Remember Hebrews 12:2 says that we are to "Look unto Jesus the author and perfecter of our faith." No man has authored your faith, nor can any man complete or perfect it.

Even when other people are not involved, the circumstances of life can get so painful that we may be tempted to "blame" God for allowing our suffering or failing to alleviate it. We allow our hearts to get hardened rather than enroll as a "student" in the "class of suffering." It is only when we repent, when we turn to God and come to this "class" as a "student" in the "school of the spirit" that we put ourselves in the only place where we can experience quite profoundly the supernatural comforting of the Holy Spirit that is promised to us (2Cor. 1:3-7).

No one can comfort and teach you like He can. Sometimes explanations won't help. Sometimes there is no answer to the question "why?" But there is always the comfort and the ministry of the Spirit available to us. Jesus told His original disciples to wait until Shavuot for the Holy Spirit to come to them and begin His ministry in their lives. This is the time of year to ask yourself these questions. Have you received the Spirit of God into your life? Do you know His power? Do you know His comfort? Are you allowing Him to do His work of transformation in your life? (Titus 3:5, Rom 12:2, 2Cor. 3:18, Col. 3:10).

The promise of Shavuot is for you! Remember the word of the Apostle Peter in Acts 2:38-39: *"Repent, and let each of you be baptized in the name of Jesus the Messiah for the forgiveness of your sins; and you shall receive the gift of the Holy Spirit. For the promise is for you and your children, and for all who are far off, as many as the Lord our God shall call to Himself."*

KINGDOM PERSPECTIVES
ON
THE LORD JESUS

Chapter 17

The Angel of the Lord

There is a very mysterious and unique person who frequently appears in the Old Testament. This person is called "the Angel of the Lord," or more literally translated "the Angel of Yehovah." The Hebrew word for angel is "Mal'ak" which means a messenger or one who is dispatched as a deputy. As we study this unique person in the Scriptures we see that although He is the messenger of God, He acts, speaks and is often referred to as God Himself. The revelation the Hebrew Scriptures declare about the Angel of the Lord gives us insight into the true nature of God. Yehovah acts and speaks as God, and the Angel of the Lord acts and speaks as God.

The first mention of the Angel of the Lord is in Genesis 16:7-13. In this passage we find Hagar, Sari's handmaiden, wandering exhausted in the wilderness, having been cast out of the home she shared with Sari and Abram. This rejected woman meets the Angel of the Lord by a spring of water, where He makes her a promise and gives her a prophecy. The Angel promises to multiply her descendants. Who has authority to make such a promise? Who has that kind of power and authority? Then the Angel prophesies to her. He proclaims that she will have a son and that she should call him "Ishmael" (God will hear). Hagar speaks to the Angel and addresses him as God. Verse 13 says that Hagar, *"called the name of Yehovah who spoke to her."* She said to the Angel, *"You are a God who sees."* In Hebrew she calls the angel *El Roi. El* is God, and *Roi* is "the seeing one." In other words, she said to the Angel of the Lord, you are "Yehovah, the God who sees."

In this first manifestation of the Angel of the Lord we see that:

- He is recognized as Yehovah,

- He is called God,

- He declares the future, and

- He makes promises that only God Himself can fulfill.

THE ANGEL OF THE LORD IS NONE OTHER THAN THE LORD GOD YEHOVAH HIMSELF!

With each successive appearance of the Angel of the Lord this revelation is confirmed. His next appearance is in Genesis 22. In verse 2, Abraham is told by the Lord to take his son up to Mount Moriah and offer him as a sacrifice. In obedience to the word of the Lord, Abraham ascends the mountain, builds an altar, binds Isaac upon it, lifts his knife and is about to slay his son, when the Angel of the Lord calls out to him. *"Abraham, Abraham, do not stretch out your hand against the lad, and do nothing to him, for now I know that you fear God, since you have not withheld your son, your only son, from ME."* We must understand that it was Yehovah who gave Abraham the command to sacrifice his son. Genesis 22:1 says that God was testing Abraham. Now it is the Angel of the Lord who says "now

I know you fear God, for you have not withheld your son from ME."

Now look at verses 15 thru 18. Then the Angel of the Lord called to Abraham a second time from heaven, and said, *"By Myself I have sworn, declares Yehovah, because you have done this thing and have not withheld your son, your only son, indeed I will greatly bless you, and I will greatly multiply your seed as the stars of the heavens and as the sand which is on the seashore; and your seed shall possess the gate of their enemies. In your seed all the nations of the earth shall be blessed, because you have obeyed My voice."* Pay close attention to how the Angel of the Lord speaks about Himself. He declares Himself to be Yehovah. It is the Angel of the Lord who said *"By Myself I have sworn, declares Yehovah ... I will greatly bless you and I will greatly multiply your seed, because you have obeyed My voice."* Whose voice? The voice of the Angel of the Lord. **The Angel of the Lord is Yehovah!**

As we continue in our study we find that Jacob, Abraham's grandson, had his own encounter with the Angel of the Lord. In order to understand this encounter, we have to compare Genesis 28:13 with Genesis 31:11-13. In Genesis 28:13 Jacob had a dream while sleeping upon a rock. In the dream he saw, *"A ladder set on the earth, with its top reaching to heaven, and the angels of God ascending and descending on it. Yehovah stood above it and said, "I am Yehovah, the God of your father Abraham and the God of Isaac. And the land on which you lie, I will give it to you and to your descendants."* Then Yehovah said the same thing the Angel of the Lord said to Abraham about their descendants. When Jacob awoke he said, *"Surely Yehovah is in this place, and I did not know it."* He was afraid and said, *"How awesome is this place! This is none other than the house of God, Beth El, and this is the gate of heaven."*

Keep in mind that in verse 13 it is Yehovah who stood above the ladder and identified Himself as Yehovah. Turn now to Genesis 31:11-13. Jacob is testifying to his wives about a different dream that he had. In this dream the Angel of the Lord speaks to him and says in verse 13, *"...I am the God of Bethel, where you anointed a pillar and where you made a vow to me ..."* In Genesis 28:13, the God of Bethel identifies Himself as *"Yehovah,"* and now in this dream the Angel of the Lord says, *"I am the God of Bethel ..."* Again we see the Angel of the Lord identifying himself as Yehovah.

In Genesis 32:24-31, we read the famous story of Jacob wrestling with a "man" all night long. This man changes Jacob's name to Israel, and Jacob seeks His blessing. Jacob calls the place where they wrestled "Peniel" (the face of God) because he said, *"I have seen God face to face yet my life was preserved."* Jacob understood that the "man" he wrestled with was "God." God was manifesting Himself in such a way that Jacob could both wrestle with Him and also understand that the one whom he wrestled was in fact God manifesting Himself as a man. Because Jacob sought to know who the man really was, he asked His name. The man did not tell Jacob His name, but blessed him. All that happened in that encounter convinced Jacob that he had in fact "seen God face to face" and had survived.

In Genesis 48, Jacob blesses his children just before his death. In verse 15 he says, *"... the God before whom my fathers Abraham and Isaac walked, the God who has been my shepherd all my life to this day, the Angel who has redeemed me from all evil, bless the lads, and may my name live on in them."* In this one sentence, Jacob clearly shows his understanding that the Angel of the Lord and God are one. In this prayer he asks that the God who has been his shepherd, and the Angel who has redeemed him from evil, bless his children. He understood the divine nature and power of the Angel that had so dramatically impacted his life. Because of that understanding he wanted to make sure that this Angel was called upon to bless his children.

Perhaps the most profound revelation we have about the nature and person of the Angel of the Lord is found in the famous story of Moses and the burning bush recorded in Exodus 3:2-6. Pay close attention to who is speaking. In verse 2 we read, *"Now Moses was pasturing a flock of Jethro, his father-in-law, the priest of Midian, and he led the flock to the west side of the wilderness and came to Horeb, the mountain of God. And the Angel of the Lord appeared to him in a blazing fire from the midst of a bush. And he looked, and behold, the bush was burning with fire, yet the bush was not consumed. So Moses said, 'I must turn aside now and see this marvelous sight, why the bush is not burned up.' And when Yehovah saw that he turned aside to look, God called to him from the midst of the bush and said, 'Moses! Moses!'"*

Verse 2 says the Angel of the Lord appeared to Moses in a blazing fire from the midst of the bush, yet verse 4 says that God called to Moses from the midst of the bush. Here again we see that the Angel of the Lord is none other than God Himself. As we continue to read in verse 7, Yehovah says, *"I have surely seen your affliction."* In verse 11, *"Moses said to God ..."* In verse 12, *"God said to Moses ..."* In verse 14, God identifies Himself and tells Moses to tell the people that, *"I AM has sent me to you."* In verse 16, God tells Moses to tell the elders that Yehovah has appeared to him. All of this reflects back to verse 3, where we are told that it was the Angel of the Lord who appeared to Moses in the burning bush. The Angel who speaks out of the burning bush speaks as Yehovah Himself. The Scripture clearly teaches us that this Angel is God. We read about

Yehovah and we read about the Angel of Yehovah, yet the clear revelation of the Hebrew Scriptures is that **this Angel is in fact Yehovah God Himself.** Whenever this Angel speaks or acts, He does so as Yehovah, as God.

Read Exodus 13:21: *"And Yehovah was going before them in a pillar of cloud by day to lead them on the way and in a pillar of fire by night to give them light, that they might travel by day and by night. Yehovah was before them in a pillar of cloud by day, and He was in a pillar of fire by night."* Who was in the pillar? Yehovah. Look now at Exodus 14:19-20. Who was in the pillar? The Angel of the Lord. *"And the Angel of God, who had been going before the camp of Israel, moved and went behind them; and the pillar of cloud moved from before them and stood behind them"* (Verse 24). *"And it came about at the morning watch that the Lord looked down on the army of the Egyptians through the pillar of fire and cloud and brought the army of the Egyptians into confusion."* Who was inside the pillar? The Angel of the Lord and Yehovah. We clearly see the plurality of God. One God in two manifestations. Yehovah speaks and acts as God; the Angel of the Lord speaks and acts as God. Both of them speak as God, both of them speak with the authority of God, both of them demonstrate the fact that they are God.

In Numbers 22, we read of the pagan prophet Balaam and his donkey. He was bribed by the Moabite king Balak to curse Israel. It was the Angel of the Lord who prevented him from doing so. In verse 25, we read that the Angel of the Lord said to him, *"Go with the men, but you shall speak only the word which I shall tell you."* Balaam, understanding who spoke to him, said in verse 38, *"... am I able to speak anything at all? The word that God puts in my mouth, that I will speak."* He knew that the Angel speaking to him was none other than God Himself.

In Judges 2:1-5, the Angel of the Lord speaks of Himself in very profound terms. Again, pay special attention to who is speaking. *"Now the Angel of the Lord came up from Gilgal to Bochim. And he said, 'I brought you up out of Egypt and led you into the land which I have sworn to your fathers; and I said, "I will never break My covenant with you, and as for you, you shall make no covenant with the inhabitants of this land; you shall tear down their altars. But you have not obeyed Me; what is this you have done?" Therefore I also said, "I will not drive them out before you; but they shall become as thorns in your sides, and their gods shall be a snare to you."' And it came about when the Angel of the Lord spoke these words to all the sons of Israel, that the people lifted up their voices and wept. So they named that place Bochim; and there they sacrificed to the Lord."*

Who brought the children of Israel out of Egypt? Who led them into the land? Who swore to their fathers? Who promised to never break His covenant with them? Who did they disobey? Certainly the answer to all of these questions is the Lord God Almighty, Yehovah Himself. Yet here the Angel of the Lord is declaring that He did all of these things! Here again, in a very profound way, we see that the Angel of the Lord is none other than Yehovah Himself. He is God!

In Gideon's encounter with the Angel of the Lord (Judges 6:11-21), the Angel again speaks as God Himself. The Scripture, in referring to the Angel of the Lord as he speaks to Gideon, says that it is Yehovah who is speaking. (The Angel is sitting under a tree talking to Gideon, an interesting way for him to speak to fearful Gideon. Was he trying to make Gideon more comfortable because he was such a timid person?) Verse 14 says, *"Yehovah looked at him and said ... "* Verse 16 says, *"Yehovah said to him ... "*

The Angel of the Lord looks and speaks, but the Bible says that it is Yehovah who is looking and speaking.

The Angel of the Lord appeared many times in ancient Israel. In 1Kings, chapter 19, we see the Angel of the Lord giving direction to the prophet. In 1Chronicles 21:18, He commands David to build an altar. In 2Samuel 24, a plague is brought upon the nation of Israel because of David's sin of taking a census. The Angel of the Lord is about to destroy Jerusalem when Yehovah calls to Him to stop. God gives David a chance to repent and offer a sacrifice. When he does, the plague ends. In 2Kings 19:35, the Angel destroys 185,000 Assyrians in one night. In Zechariah 1:12, we see the Angel of the Lord interceding in prayer for Jerusalem. In Judges 13, the Angel appeared as a man and prophesied to Samson's parents about his birth and life.

In commenting about Psalm 40:7—*"Lo, in the volume of the Book it is written of Me"*—Hebrews 10:7 tells us that that verse is speaking about Jesus. As we study the New Testament revelation about the Person of the Lord Jesus, I believe we can clearly draw the conclusion that the Angel of the Lord is a Theophany, or a Christophany, that is, a pre-incarnate manifestation of the Lord Jesus. We can see the parallels between Jesus and the Angel of the Lord. For example in John 8:58, when speaking about Himself to the Jewish leaders Jesus said, *"Before Abraham was I AM."* By using that exact expression, Jesus made reference to the revelation God gave about Himself to Moses in the burning bush. As we saw earlier, the one who appeared to Moses and called Himself the "I AM" was the Angel of the Lord. By making this statement, Jesus was clearly declaring that he was the "I AM." The Jewish leaders understood that this is what Jesus meant and it made them so angry that they wanted to stone him.

Jesus was identifying Himself as the Angel of the Lord. The Angel was the one sent by God yet was God Himself. He was the one sent by God, yet with the power and the authority to act and speak as God. The Angel of the Lord expressed and demonstrated His deity; so did the Lord Jesus during His earthly ministry. When Jesus said, *"The Father and I are one"* (John 10:30), He was not creating a new theological doctrine about His own divine nature or the nature of God. He was speaking about concepts the Jewish Bible scholars of His day had read and studied in their own Holy Scriptures.

Even though they had not interpreted their Scriptures to teach the concept of a divine Messiah appearing in human form, they had in fact read about it in their Bible. They just never understood it in the way Jesus, and then the Apostles, acknowledged it. This was why Jesus told them in John 5:39, *"You study the Scriptures because you think that in them you have eternal life, but it is they that testify of me!"* What an awesome statement for Jesus to make about Himself. He declared that the Holy Torah, Prophets, and Psalms all give evidence about, and bear witness to, Him!

In Luke 24, beginning with verse 13, we read about Jesus testifying to two forlorn disciples on the road to Emmaus. In verse 26 Jesus said to them, *"Ought not the Messiah to have suffered these things and to enter into His glory? And beginning at Moses and all the Prophets, He expounded to them in all the Scriptures the things concerning Himself."* This is why the writer of the Book of Hebrews quotes Psalm 40:7, in declaring that all of the Hebrew Scriptures are written about Jesus.

As we study the unique person of the Angel of the Lord, we gain insight into the God who reveals Himself to us in the pages of the Hebrew Bible. The Angel of the Lord shows us aspects of the true nature of the God of Israel. As we study the New Testament teachings about Messiah Jesus, we can understand that He really is Emmanuel, God With Us (Isaiah 7:14, Matthew 1:23). Our faith is greatly strengthened when we come to the realization that the continual unfolding of revelation in the pages of the Bible brings us an exalted vision of Jesus.

We can see why the New Testament refers to Him as the Lord Jesus. As we see HIM described in the pages of the Old Testament, our faith in the writings of the New Testament increases. We realize that what Jesus said about Himself, and what the Apostles wrote about Him, are squarely founded on the revelation that God gave centuries earlier. Truly we can see that throughout the Hebrew Scriptures it is written of Jesus, because they testify of Him. Who is this mysterious person, the Angel of the Lord? He is none other than the Messiah of Israel, the Lord Jesus Himself!

Chapter 18

The Deity of the Messiah

A study in the scriptures

Write out these verses. Take time to study and meditate on them. Recognizing who Jesus really is will strengthen your faith and greatly empower your life in God.

JESUS IS GOD
    John 1:1

JESUS IS CALLED GOD
    Isa. 9:6

    Jer. 23:6

    Matt. 1:23

    John 1:1 20:28

    Titus 2:13

    Heb.1:8

    2Peter 1:1

Jesus is called Lord - "Kurios"
Luke 2:11, 19:34

John 4:1, 6:23, 11:2, 20:2,13,18,20,25, 21:7

Acts 9:17, 10:36

Isa. 9:6

1 Cor.2:8 (compare with Ps. 24:8-10)

Heb. 1:8 (compare with Ps. 45:6-7)

Divine Titles Of Jesus
Emmanuel - God with us - Matt. 1:23

Lord of All - Acts 10:36

Lord of Glory - 1 Cor. 2:8

Everlasting Father, Almighty God - Isa. 9:6

The Lord's Messiah - Luke 2:26

The Son of God - Matt. 3:17

The Only Begotten Son - John 1:18, 3:16,18, 1 John 4:9

Alpha and Omega - Rev. 22:13

The Lord - Acts 9:17

Son of the Highest - Luke 1:32

Son of the Blessed - Mark 14:61

The Bread of God - John 6:33

The Holy One of God - Mark 1:24

King of Kings & Lord of Lords - Rev.19:16

Lord and Savior - 2Peter 3:2

The Word of God - Rev. 19:13

DIVINE CHARACTER IS ASCRIBED TO HIM

Holy by birth - Luke 1:35

Righteous - Isa. 53:11, Heb. 1:9

Faithful - Isa. 11:5, 1 Thess. 5:24

Truth - John 1:14,14:6

Just - John 5:30

Guileless - 1 Peter 2:22

Sinless - 2Cor. 5:21

Spotless - 1 Peter 1:19

Innocent - Matt. 27:4

DIVINE WORSHIP GIVEN TO HIM

Matt. 2:2,11, 4:9-10, 8:2, 9:18, 14:33, 15:25, 18:26,

28:9,17

Mark 5:6

Luke 24:52

John 5:23, 9:38

Acts 7:59,10:25-6,14:13-15

Rom. 10:13

Heb. 1:6

Rev. 5:9-10, 7:10

DIVINE OFFICES ARE ASCRIBED TO HIM

Creator - John 1:3, Col. 1:16, Heb 1:1-3

Mediator - 1 Tim. 2:5, Heb. 8:6

Head of the Church - Eph. 1:22, Col. 1:15

Savior - 2Pet. 3:2

Judge - 2Tim. 4:1

Preserver - Heb. 1:3

Resurrection and life - John 11:25

Messenger of the Covenant - Malachi 3:1

THE WORKS OF GOD ARE ASCRIBED TO HIM

He is omnipresent - Matt. 18:20, 28:20, 2Cor. 13:5,

Eph.1:23

He is the creator - John 1:3, Col. 1:15-18, Heb. 1:10

He raises the dead - John 5:25

He rules over the universe - Rev. 3:14

He forgives sin - Luke 5:21, 7:48, Mark 2:5-10

He knows the hearts of all men - Mk. 2:8, Lk. 5:22, Jn. 2:24

He judges men - 2Tim. 4:1, Rev. 6:10

God Is A Tri-Unity

Gen. 1:26, 11:7, 19:24

Psalm 45:6-7

Isa. 6:8, 9:6-7, 48:16

John 1:1

Phil. 2:6

Heb. 1:5-12

1 John 5:7

Rev.1:8, 22:13

JESUS IS MENTIONED AS PART OF THE GODHEAD
Matt. 28:19

John 5:19-23,14:1,23,17:3

Rom. 1:7

2Cor. 13:14

1 John 5:7-8 and Rev. 5:13

JESUS HAD AN ETERNAL PRE-EXISTENCE
Micah 5:1-2

Isa. 7:14, 9:6

John 1:1-2, John 1:15, 8:58, 17:5

Heb. 1:8

Col. 1:17

Phil. 2:6

Rev.1:8, 2:8, 22:13

THE ANGEL OF THE LORD
  Speaks And Acts As Jehovah Himself

Gen. 16:7-13

Gen. 21:17-18

Gen. 22:11-18

Gen. 31:11-13

Ex. 3:2-4:18

Jud. 6:11-24

Jud. 13:3-21

1 Chr. 21:16-17

HE IS DECLARED TO BE THE SON OF GOD BY:
  God - Matt. 3:17,17:5 Mark 9:7

Himself - John 10:36

Angels - Luke 1:32-35

Demons - Matt. 8:29, Luke 4:41

John the Baptist - John 1:34

His Disciples - Matt. 14:33

Peter - Matt. 16:16, John 6:69

John - John 20:31

Mark - Mark 1:1

Paul - Acts 9:20, Gal. 2:20

Martha - John 11:27

Nathaniel - John 1:49

Ethiopian Eunuch - Acts 8:37

Roman Centurion - Matt. 27:54

HE IS THE ONLY BEGOTTEN SON OF GOD
John 1:14,18

John 3:16-18

Acts 13:33

Heb. 1:5, 5:5, 11:7

1 John 4:9

HIS ENEMIES UNDERSTOOD HIS CLAIM TO BE THE SON OF GOD
Satan - Matt. 4:3-6

The Crowds - Matt. 27:40-43

The Jewish Leaders - John 19:7

JESUS' PERSONAL CLAIMS TO DEITY
John 8:58   "Before Abraham was born, I am."

John 10:11,14   "I am the good shepherd."

John 6:35,41,48 "I am the bread of life."

John 6:51   "I am the living bread.."

John 8:12, 9:5 "I am the light of the world."

John 10:7,9   "I am the door for the sheep."

John 11:25 - "I am the resurrection and the life."

John 14:6 - "I am the way and the truth and the life."

John 15:1,5 - "I am the true vine."

John 10:36 - "I am the Son of God."

Revelation 1:17 - "I am the first and the last"

JESUS AND JEHOVAH OFTEN MENTIONED IN TANDEM

2Cor. 13:14 - The grace of the Lord Jesus Christ, and the love of God, and the communion of the Holy Ghost, be with you all. Amen.

Matt. 28:19 - Go ye therefore, and teach all nations, baptizing them in the name of the Father, and of the Son, and of the Holy Ghost.

1 Thess. 3:11 - Now God himself and our Father, and our Lord Jesus Christ, direct our way unto you.

1 Cor. 12:4-6 - Now there are diversities of gifts, but the same Spirit. And there are differences of administrations, but the same Lord. And there are diversities of operations, but it is the same God which worketh all in all.

Titus 3:4-5 - But after that the kindness and love of God our Savior toward man appeared, Not by works of righteousness which we have done, but according to His mercy he saved us, by the washing of regeneration, and renewing of the Holy Ghost.

Rom. 1:7 - To all that be in Rome, beloved of God, called to be saints: Grace to you and peace from God our Father, and the Lord Jesus Christ.

James 1:1 - James, a servant of God and of the Lord Jesus Christ, to the twelve tribes which are scattered abroad, greeting.

John 14:23 - Jesus answered and said unto him, "If a man loves me, he will keep my words: and my Father will love him, and we will come unto him, and make our abode with him."

JESUS IS JEHOVAH

Ps. 102:25-27 - Jehovah called the creator who never changes

Heb. 1:10-12 - Jesus called the creator who never changes

Isa. 40:3-4 - Make straight the path of Jehovah

Matt. 3:3, Luke 1:68,69,76 - Make straight the path of Jesus

Jer. 11:20, 17:10 - Jehovah tests hearts

Rev. 2:23 - Jesus tests hearts

Isa. 6:1,3,10 - Isaiah saw Jehovah's glory

John 12:37-41 - Isaiah saw Jesus' glory

Isa. 8:13-14 - Jehovah is the stone of stumbling

1 Peter 2:7,8 - Jesus is the stone of stumbling

Isa. 40:10-11

Ezekiel 34:11,12,18 - Jehovah is the Shepherd

John 10:11 Luke 19:10 - Jesus is the Shepherd

Jer. 17:5-7 - Believe and trust only in Jehovah

John 14:1 - Believe and trust only in Jesus

Isa. 45:23 - Knees bow and tongues confess Jehovah is Lord

Phil. 2:11 - Knees bow and tongues confess Jesus is Lord

Isa. 43:11, 45:21, Hosea 13:4 - Jehovah is the savior

Titus 2:13, 2Peter 1:1, Acts 2:21 - Jesus is the savior

Isa. 44:6,8 - Jehovah is the first and the last

Rev. 1:11,17, 2:8, 22:13 - Jesus is the first and the last

Ex. 3:14, Deut. 32:39, Isa. 43:10 - Jehovah is the great I Am

John 8:24,58, 13:19, 18:5 - Jesus is the great I Am

Deut. 10:17, Psalm 136:1-3 - Jehovah is the Lord of Lords and King of Kings

Rev. 17:14, 19:16, 1 Tim. 6:14-16 - Jesus is the Lord of Lords and King of Kings

Ps. 27:1, Isa.60:20, Micah 7:8 - Jehovah is the Light

Luke 2:32, John 1:9, John 8:12 - Jesus is the Light

Gen.18:25, Joel 3:12 - Jehovah is the Judge

Rom. 14:10, 2Cor. 5:10, 2Tim. 4:1 - Jesus is the Judge

Gen. 18:1,14, Isa. 43:10,44:24, Jer. 32:18 - Jehovah is God

Jn 1:1,20:28, 2Pet. 1:1, Ti. 2:13, Heb. 1:8 - Jesus is God

TRACTS FOR
SHARING YOUR FAITH

You may reproduce these tracts in any form

for your personal witness.

Chapter 19

The Resurrection of Jesus:
Hoax or History

Imagine yourself a judge facing a courtroom filled with attentive spectators. They are intently listening for your verdict as you weigh the facts presented by the prestigious attorney. He speaks to you: "The issue before you, your honor, is the case of the Resurrection of Jesus. Was it a hoax? Or is it history? Your honor, you must base your decision upon the evidence presented. We expect you to be impartial, to weigh the facts as they are without prejudice."

Please remember this, the meaning of the resurrection is a theological matter, but the fact of the resurrection is a historical matter. The question must be decided upon by the historical evidence.

WHO ARE OUR WITNESSES?

In evaluating evidence, we must consider not only what the witness says but also his character and his trustworthiness. Ancient historians were usually paid by royalty who desired to be flattered. They were not motivated to make truth known. The New Testament writers were not paid by anyone. On the contrary, they risked loss of liberty and even death for what they wrote. No impartial court could lightly dismiss the evidence of witnesses ready to suffer such hardships for what they assert. They declare unanimously that they saw, heard, and touched the reality of Jesus' resurrection. If we trust pagan historians whose motives must be suspect, why not trust historians whose motives are pure—as evidenced by their willingness to suffer for their testimony.

We have only three options when it comes to examining the disciples' trustworthiness as eyewitnesses:

1) They were all liars motivated by some evil desire.

2) They themselves were deceived.

3) Their testimony is the truth.

1. Would liars knowingly preach that which would bring them hardship, suffering, persecution, torture, and death? Not likely! Liars would proclaim that which would ensure their own comfort and prosperity. Liars would even change their message to avoid negative responses, yet the disciples adamantly proclaimed the resurrection message despite the reaction it brought.

2. Could they have been deceived? Many have said that they all suffered hallucinations wanting to see Jesus so badly. But the nature of a hallucination is that it distorts understanding and brings confusion. It does not bring positive transformation as in the case of the disciples. Hallucinations never work to integrate a personality—they are signs of personality disintegration, i.e., psychosis—and certainly never impart a new hope, positive motivation, and fearlessness. Before the resurrection the disciples were confused cowards; afterwards they were confident and fearless.

Moreover, these men were not likely candidates for such mental confusion. They were practical, down-to-earth, hardworking fishermen, pragmatic businessmen, skeptics themselves, whose lack of faith and other character flaws were often rebuked by Jesus himself. At the first hearing of the resurrection, none of them believed. Only after personal encounters with the resurrected Jesus, did they believe.

3. The disciples report that at different times and places, sometimes together, sometimes apart, they had very similar experiences. The nature of hallucinations is not like this. Each hallucination would be as different in nature as the men themselves. They would not have uniform experience. They report that they talked to, listened to, ate with, and even touched the Resurrected Jesus. When eleven men have the same distinct, detailed experiences with the same resulting transformations, how can they be mental delusions? Would not one of them doubt the 'reality' of his experience under the pressures of intense persecution? But they knew the reality of these experiences. They could not doubt. Therefore, the only logical conclusion we can come to is that the disciples were not liars and they were not deceived. They simply told the truth of their experiences. Jesus rose from the dead!

WHAT IS THE TESTIMONY OF OUR WITNESSES?

Their testimony is simple and straightforward:

A) Jesus died.

B) He was buried.

C) On the third day He rose bodily from the dead.

Let us examine these three events.

A) Jesus died.

Unless Jesus actually was dead when taken from the cross, there would be no resurrection, only a hoax. The eyewitness testimony is that:

1. Jesus was scourged with a flagellum (an instrument of torture consisting of long stripes of leather with sharp pieces of bone and metal attached to rip the flesh) by Roman soldiers who were notoriously cruel. The account shows that He was so badly beaten that He needed help to carry His own cross.

2. Jesus was mocked. This consisted of cursing, blaspheming, spitting, beard pulling, and a crown of extremely long thorns being jammed on His head. These would cause great emotional and psychological pain that would intensify the physical pain caused by the scourging. The mental anguish caused by mocking should not be minimized. The emotional distress that was caused by being naked, mocked by the crowd, and deserted by His disciples (except two women and John) would further rob Him of strength. Is it no wonder that He cried out, "My God, My God, why have You forsaken me?"

3. He was forced to carry His own cross. This caused more bleeding from shoulder wounds, and also drained even more of His strength.

4. He was nailed to the cross at the wrists and feet, and He was also pierced through the chest by a spear. These obviously would not only cause intense pain, but a great loss of blood.

Is it possible that anyone could survive such an ordeal?

That all these factors culminated in Jesus' death is certified by a number of witnesses. The Roman executioners were professionals who knew when a man was dead. For them to testify that a victim was dead when in fact he was not would make them liable to be executed themselves. They would therefore not easily make a mistake. Because Jesus died so rapidly, Pilate questioned the centurion in charge of the crucifixion to be sure that Jesus had actually died. Pilate believed this report and gave Joseph of Aramathea permission to bury Jesus. Proof that the centurion knew Jesus to be dead was that he did not order Jesus' legs to be broken (to hasten His death), as he did to the two thieves who were crucified with Him.

Joseph of Aramathea, and those involved in placing the body in the tomb, did not doubt that Jesus was dead. If they did, they would not have prepared him for burial, they would have sought medical help.

B) Jesus was buried.

Our witnesses testify to the following facts. Jesus was anointed with various burial spices, put in burial wrappings, and laid in a cave-like tomb. The entrance to the tomb was blocked by a large stone rolled in place. The stone was then fixed with a seal and a group of soldiers were set to guard the tomb. The soldiers were insurance against anyone moving the stone; the seal, insurance against the soldiers entering the tomb.

C) The tomb is open. The body of Jesus is gone!

On Sunday morning the tomb was empty. The stone was rolled away and the seal broken. No one could be found to argue against these points. The tomb was open —the body of Jesus was gone. The tomb was not empty, however. Left inside the tomb were the grave clothes. This is an interesting piece of evidence. If Jesus was not dead when taken off the cross and only appeared to be dead, could He manage to revive in a cold, dark, damp tomb? Would He have had the strength to remove His wrappings? If He did have the strength, why bother to do it? He had no clothes and His body was lacerated from head to foot. How would a man beaten almost to death, then nailed to a cross, thrust through with a spear, move a huge stone (weighing perhaps two tons) and then sneak past trained soldiers? It takes more faith to believe that than it does to believe that the Almighty could raise Jesus from the dead.

The grave clothes are proof of the resurrection in another way. Who would steal the body and leave the wrappings? Why bother to waste time unwrapping the body? The disciples saw the grave clothes as a testimony to the resurrection. They were in the tomb, Jesus was not. He simply, in His resurrected body, passed through the grave clothes as easily as He passed through walls. And what about the guards? Did they sleep at the risk of their own lives? And if they did sleep, how could they testify about what happened while they slept?

This then is the disciples' testimony. Jesus died, was buried and on the third day rose from the dead.

What Happened to the Body of Jesus?
We have only five options open to us.

1.   The Disciples stole the body.

2.   The Jews stole the body.

3.   The Romans stole the body.

4.   Jesus escaped.

5.   Jesus was resurrected.

LET US EXAMINE THESE OPTIONS.

1. The disciples had no motive for stealing the body. Why would they steal it, and then proclaim at the risk of life, limb and liberty, that He had risen from the dead? Why would they die for a lie that they themselves had fabricated? Obviously they would not. They themselves gained nothing except pain, suffering, and ultimately, martyrdom for the message preached.

2. The Jewish authorities had no motives to move the body; they would only want to produce the corpse. This would have ended any "resurrection" preaching. But since no corpse had been discovered, or could be, all that could be done was to start a rumor that the disciples stole the body.

3. The Romans also had no motive. Why would they steal it? Why would they crucify Him and then steal His body? For what possible reason? To confuse the disciples? To agitate the Jews? They would rather Jesus stay dead and cause no more trouble.

4. Some say Jesus did not die on the cross but that He merely 'swooned' into a state that appeared like death. He then recovered in the tomb and escaped. We covered this possibility in the previous section and saw that it was impossible.

After considering all of the above FACTS, we have come to the inevitable conclusion that what turned the disciples from fearful cowards into fearless apostles was nothing less than an encounter with the resurrected Messiah Himself. The apostles testify that this is precisely what happened. That these men were radically transformed is evident from their impact on the First Century world. Their influence, through the pages of the New Testament, is still felt today. They began to preach their message right in Jerusalem where the crucifixion took place, not in some far away city where no one had ever heard of Jesus. They were now bold as to preach right in the faces of those who threatened them with punishment and death, those who earlier caused them to cower in fear.

No one could produce a corpse because there was no corpse to produce. Jesus was alive from the dead and the disciples knew it. They had good news to tell everyone and began to do just that.

What Can The Resurrection Mean To Me?

The good news of the resurrection is simply this: God, the creator, loves each one of us dearly. He wants to share all of His vast creation with us. He wants to share His life, His heart, His wealth, and more importantly, His love with us. But He could not because our sins separated us from Him; so in order to bridge the gap created by sin, God devised a plan, in which His son, who never sinned, would take the punishment due us for our sins. (Read Isaiah Chapter 53.) God could now say to everyone who believes in Jesus and receives Him as Lord and Savior (i.e., the one who saves them from sin) that He no longer rejects them because of their sins but now accepts them because they have the one who takes their sins away. Now God's love can be expressed to us personally. We can receive the inheritance that God wants to give us. We can begin to experience heaven on earth.

Wouldn't you like to enter into a personal love relationship with God? Wouldn't you like to enter your spiritual inheritance? It's easy to do, God never makes things difficult. Just be willing to repent, that is, turn away from any known sins, things you know are wrong or are contrary to what the Bible teaches.

If you open your heart to pray the following prayer sincerely, Jesus will come into your life by the power of the Holy Spirit. You will begin to experience His life, His love, His joy, and His peace. He will lead you to a Church where there are authentic and sincere believers who can help you grow in the Lord. Get a Bible and read a portion of it everyday. The Bible is an amazing book, it has the ability to feed your spirit and build your faith. Pray every day; tell the Lord in your own words about the things going on in your life. Watch God answer your prayers.

If you are sincere with God, He will be sincere with you and will manifest Himself to you. Now all you have to do is pray this prayer:

Heavenly Father, I thank you that you love me and sent your son Jesus to die on the cross, and shed His blood as payment for my sins. I believe that Jesus did actually rise from the dead and is now alive! Lord Jesus, thank you for dying for my sins, and rising again. I open my heart to you and ask you to come into my heart, come into my life and become my Lord and Savior. Fill me with your Holy Spirit so that I will have the ability and the power to follow you, obey your voice, and your written word, the Bible.

In Jesus' Name, Amen

Chapter 20

Please Allow Me to Introduce You to Jesus

I have found that the Divine artist who conceived and created all the pleasures of the natural world, and mankind with the sensational ability to enjoy those pleasures, is a lover, who, like all lovers, desires to be freely loved in return. He desires that those He loves reciprocate that love freely and willingly, not because they feel forced to. A love relationship is not created by feelings of guilt for not attending religious services. Saying memorized but lifeless prayers is not pleasing to God. Neither is obeying little understood commandments or traditions because of fear of community censure, parental scorn, or eternal damnation.

Love is birthed and grows in a mutually shared relationship, an ongoing giving and receiving of oneself and one's affection. This dynamic of "love" that all people need so deeply is also a reflection of the nature and personality of the One who created mankind with the ability to give, and the need for, mutually shared love and affection. Without love, life shrivels up into an abyss of darkness, depression, despair, and ultimately death. When children are deprived of love, they grow up to be haters of themselves and everyone else. When adults are deprived of love, they turn against everyone and then ultimately against themselves. But when love comes into your life, everything changes; darkness to light, depression to joy, despair to hope, and death to life.

Ultimately the issue of God and His reality in your life boils down to this issue of love. Do you want the power of God's love in your life or do you want to live apart from that power and that love? No religion, Church, synagogue, mosque, tradition, holy book, person, or ritual can give you that love or that power. There is only one way for you to experience God's love and power in your life. This life changing experience begins when you are willing to ask for and be open to a revelation of it.

You can have the greatest sex life, or all the money, fame, or power in the world, but that will not bring you all that you were created for. You were created for more than natural pleasures. You were created to experience the untold pleasures of a personal relationship with the Divine pleasure giver.

I want to share with you a spiritual secret that completely revolutionized my life: "Revelation is the key to entering into a personal relationship with God. Prayer is the key to revelation, and Jesus the Messiah is the key to answered prayer"!

You might ask why Jesus, and not Buddha, Mohammed, Moses or some other ancient or modern spiritual teacher. The answer is based on believing the writings of the ancient prophets recorded in the Old Testament, and the eyewitness accounts of the writers of the New Testament. Those prophets clearly showed, hundreds of years beforehand, how we would be able to recognize the true Messiah when he came. The New Testament writings teach how you can personally experience the love and power of God through what the Messiah did when He came to earth.

THE PROPHETS WROTE THAT THE MESSIAH WOULD:

1) Be born of a virgin. The book of Isaiah, chapter 7 verse 14

2) Be born in Bethlehem. The book of Micah, chapter 5 verse 2

3) Be the incarnation of God. That means that the Messiah would be God in human form. The book of Isaiah, chapter 9 verse 6

4) He would live a sinless life. The book of Isaiah, chapter 53

5) He would die as an atonement for our sins. This means that He would take our sins onto His own body so that our sins would no longer separate us from God. The book of Isaiah, chapter 53

6) He would rise from the dead. The book of Isaiah, chapter 53, and the book of Psalms, chapter 16 verse 10

7) He would send the Holy Spirit to be our helper and guide for all the affairs of our life. The book of Joel, chapter 2 verse 28

The writers of the New Testament present to you the fact that God's message about Jesus will absolutely change your life, if you open your heart to believe it. The message of the New Testament is very simple. It is this. Jesus, who is the creator, came to earth in the form of a man to show us what God is really like. He taught that sin has separated us from a personal, intimate relationship with God. He explained that sin was not just doing wrong things, but that it is a spiritual power that separates us from God and abandons us to our own devices to meet our own needs.

He taught us that He, the true Son of God, Messiah, and Savior, would die in our place. He would take our sins upon His body while on the cross, and through His death he would not only forgive our sins but also break the power of sin over our life. He taught that because He rose again from the dead we could join Him in the power of His resurrected life. He explained that the only way for you to personally experience this love and power is by opening your heart to believe in Him and His words.

This is all it will take for you to experience the reality of God. This is the simplicity of the spiritual dynamic that will change your life. If you open your heart to receive the Lord Jesus, He will take away your sins and break the power of sin over your life. In very practical terms, this means that all of the negative emotional, psychological, and physical dynamics in your life will no longer control you.

As you join your life to Jesus, He will share with you His great love, wisdom, and power. As you allow His life to mix with your life, you will grow into greater and greater levels of personal freedom, love, and joy. You will in fact come to know and experience the personal peace and power that only Jesus can give.

Why will he do this? Simply because God Loves You and wants to share His life with you. Only when you personally experience this love will you be able to understand it. It is not an intellectual understanding but a deeply personal experience. If you will sincerely pray and ask God to reveal to you His reality and the truth of these facts about Jesus, I know that He will give you personal revelation that will convince you of the truth of this message. You will come to understand that when Jesus died and rose again, He did it for you. He did it so that the spiritual powers that work against you can be broken. He did it so that you could share in the same relationship with God that He has. He did it so that you can share in His spiritual wealth, not only in Heaven, but here on Earth as well.

This new life is what Jesus called being "born from above" (this is also referred to as being "born-again," read in the New Testament the gospel of John chapter 3). This new life is wonderful. It is not religion or just going to Church (although you will find yourself really enjoying Churches that are filled with God's love and power). It is simply entering into a personal relationship with God. God will adopt you and truly be your Heavenly Father. He will show you how much He genuinely loves you and wants to be a good "Daddy" to you. He will lead you, guide you, provide for you, and answer your prayers. You will find new desires filling your heart and mind. God will give you a desire to read the Bible, because you will find within its pages wonderful treasures of wisdom, knowledge, and power for living.

The greatest thing you can ever do is to enter into a personal relationship with God. Not only will He give you personal power to succeed in all areas of your life, He will also impart to you His great peace and love. He will fill your life with great joy. He will increase the quality of your life in so many ways that I cannot begin to describe them.

Perhaps you have never prayed before, but you desire to experience the love and power of God in your life. If the following prayer expresses the desires of your heart, then all you have to do is sincerely say it to God. Remember, He is a lover. He loves you and only wants to know if you really desire to come into a relationship with Him. That is all He is looking for. If you are willing to repent of your sins, that is, to turn from of your sins, then any and all problems you might have are irrelevant.

Any "sins" you may have committed are also irrelevant. They do not matter to God. He has provided a way to erase the sins of your past (through the death, burial and resurrection of Jesus) and to give you power to live a life in harmony with Him. All you have to do is sincerely want to know Him and be willing to turn away from your sins and turn toward God. He will give you the power to overcome all the problems and difficulties in your life.

YOU CAN ENTER INTO YOUR NEW LIFE WITH THE LORD BY PRAYING THIS PRAYER:

"My Heavenly Father, I want to know you and enter into a personal relationship with you. I want to experience your love and power in my life. I want to be a person who experiences your pleasures and gives you pleasure in return. Please give me a revelation of your reality in my life. Show me the truth about Jesus, so that I might understand that believing in Him and receiving Him into my heart and life, takes away my sins, gives me the great gift of the Holy Spirit, and brings me into this personal relationship with you. I want to receive your love and power into my life, so I open my heart and I open my life to you."

If you have sincerely prayed this prayer and want to grow in your new relationship with God, begin to read the Bible. God will speak to you through its pages. Don't concern yourself with things you don't yet understand. As you grow in the knowledge of God, He will answer your questions. Find a Church where there are true believers (not just Church goers) and there you will find new friends to encourage, teach, and help you. You can find out if they are true believers by asking this one simple question. "Do you have a personal relationship with Jesus?" If they look at you funny or give an unsure answer, then they have not been born again themselves. Anyone who has been truly born again will always answer that question with a very enthusiastic and confident YES!

My testimony, and the testimony of millions of others through the ages, is that Life with Jesus is wonderful. Open your heart to a personal relationship with Jesus. My heart's desire is that you will take advantage of this opportunity … You will never be the same!

"A NEW SPIRIT, A NEW LIFE!"

Chapter 21

My Personal Salvation Testimony

"SEX" "DRUGS" "ROCK AND ROLL"!

These themes consumed me while waiting for my friends. I wondered, "Who has what today?" The Hunter College cafeteria buzzed with pre-holiday excitement. Suddenly two strangers approached me. One asked, "Can we talk to you?"

"Sure," I said, "I'll talk to anyone about anything." I had no idea that my openness would completely change my life. I didn't know that my answer would open a door I never knew existed. He said, "I want to talk to you about Jesus." Being open to spiritual things, as I enjoyed occasional late night heavy "religious rap sessions," I said "Sure, go ahead. Tell me about Jesus."

At some time during our discussion, I began to review my life up to that point. I was born into a typical modern Jewish home. We observed many traditions, including having a kosher household. Not being overly religious, we attended synagogue only on the high holy days and every year had a Passover Seder (ritual meal). At age 13, I had my Bar Mitzvah, the traditional Jewish "rite-of-passage" into adulthood.

My childhood and teenage years revolved around school, sports, and girls. It was pleasant enough, with the expected adolescent difficulties, but nothing terribly traumatic. At 17, my friends and I became "hippies" and hedonists, interested only in women and getting high. During my senior year at Hunter College in New York City, having continued consistently to 'turn on,' I slowly began to realize that my life was, in fact, 'turning off.' But I was powerless to stop it. Besides, where could or would I go—no one had a better way.

It was with this perspective in mind that I maintained our conversation. As we continued, it became clear to me that what I was hearing about Jesus was the truth. I felt God's Spirit all around us and a startling vision engaged my mind. I saw myself as a man drowning in a vast ocean and passing nearby was a large ocean liner. The captain of the ship called to me from the bow, "Howie, I'll throw you a life preserver and save you. But if you don't take it, I won't take responsibility for what will happen to you next." This mental picture completely stunned me. I knew God was speaking to me and that I had a choice to make.

I was given a little booklet that had a prayer on the back page. Later, as I sat in a crowded subway a small, inner voice began to speak. "Howie, read the prayer. Read the prayer now!" Very insistently and persistently, the voice repeated its message to me quite a few times. "O.K." I whispered to the voice, "I'll read the prayer." So I took the booklet out of my back pocket and read a prayer similar to this:

"Lord Jesus, I need You. Thank You for dying on the cross for my sins. I open the door of my life and receive You as my savior and Lord. Thank You for forgiving my sins and giving me eternal life. Take control of my life. Make me the kind of person You want me to be."

The instant I finished praying, a burst of light exploded within my being. I could actually see it within myself. I felt dark forces leave my body. A tremendous, overwhelming surge of joy and peace flooded my being along with a fantastic sense of well-being. I knew that I had touched God, that He was real, and that Jesus was alive! The next morning, that same sense of well-being remained. It was not at all like the drug induced highs that always left me feeling terrible. This awareness did not leave, but continued to flow effortlessly through me.

For the first time in years I had both a clear mind and a happy heart. Indeed a heart full of JOY! Over the next weeks and months, my mind was plagued by many doubts and questions about various issues that I had never even considered before (God, the Bible, Heaven-Hell, Judaism, Tradition, Israel, Christianity, Jesus, Church, etc.), but my heart was continually filled with great joy and peace. Many people mocked me and rejected my testimony but that never dented the sense of peace and joy deep inside me. I realized that this was the LIFE OF GOD flowing in me, that He was with me, and all I had to do was follow the Bible's admonition to trust and obey. He would take care of all the rest. Indeed He has!!!

Over the years, through various times of good and bad, hard and easy, God's great peace and joy has never left. He has led me down different paths and brought me into His work as an international Bible teacher. He supernaturally sent me my wife Janet, and gave us three beautiful daughters.

Jesus will change your life if you sincerely desire it. You must repent, that is, turn away from all known sins, turn to Jesus, trust and follow Him. Then you too will find a new spirit and a new life. Pray the prayer as I did! You may not have the same initial experience, but Jesus will reveal Himself to you, forgive you, and give you the gift of the Holy Spirit!

For more information about Dr. Morgan's teaching materials, please contact our offices, or visit us online at HMMin.com

Howard Morgan Ministries

PO Box 956486

Duluth, GA 30095

770-734-0044